The Making of A Beggar:

Rejecting Personal Responsibility

Nick Buckley MBE

The Making of A Beggar:

Rejecting Personal Responsibility

Nick Buckley MBE

Academica Press
Washington~London

Library of Congress Cataloging-in-Publication Data

Names: Buckley, Nick (author)
Title: The making of a beggar : rejecting personal responsibility | Buckley, Nick
Description: Washington : Academica Press, 2022. | Includes references.
Identifiers: LCCN 2022944781 | ISBN 9781680536799 (hardcover) |
9781680536805 (paperback) | 9781680536812 (e-book)

Also by the author:

Lessons in Courage:
How I Fought Back
Against Cancel Culture and Won

The author also writes articles on many
social topics and publishes them online at
substack.com, where you can sign up for free.

Dedicated to my wife

When I am consumed by logic in the pursuit of a better tomorrow she always reminds me that the individual is the most important aspect of my work.

She helps me walk the narrow line of achieving the greatest good while protecting the voiceless and vulnerable.

Contents

You cannot hold your head high with your hand out.

- proverb

I. Introduction

My first book was easy to write, it just flowed. The last two chapters took a while to formulate, but they came together naturally as the book developed. Starting to write on day one was easy because I had a story to tell and I wanted to tell it. The words tumbled out of me as I typed. It was therapeutic. I had been traumatised. My life had changed forever. I had been betrayed. The book was my way of seeking cheap psychiatric help to overcome my life falling apart. I wrote partly out of anger and partly to understand what had happened.

Writing this book was different. There was no anger inside me. No story that desperately needed to be told. Just me and my opinions. I knew I wanted the book to explore begging and how this act permeates throughout society, but I did not know how to start.

I made some notes on potential chapter headings, real-life case studies and my own personal experience. But a spark was missing that was needed to ignite the story. The book must be a story if I expect people to read it.

It was a cold afternoon when I found the spark. I visited my mum in South Manchester, as I do on a weekly basis - hey, I am a good son! This was always a good opportunity to call into Lidl supermarket for some shopping and to stock up on everyday items and alcohol. I live in the city centre so stocking up when possible saves me a small fortune.

I drove to Lidl. I stopped at the traffic lights as they were on red. I could see the supermarket opposite. A petite white woman dressed in black tracksuit bottoms and a coat was weaving in and out of the waiting cars. She had a paper cup in her hand. She walked up to the driver's windows and shook the cup while looking pitiful. I would guess she was in her late twenties, which means she was probably very early twenties or late teens. This lifestyle has an ageing effect. Begging at traffic lights was something new in Manchester. I had started to notice it about a year before. Had fewer people walking around on the streets due to Covid led to this new practice? *Unintended consequences.*

I remember at one of my old jobs arranging for the police to clamp down on Eastern Europeans cleaning windscreens at traffic lights in the city centre. We called them *'squeegees'* after the handheld rubber tool that was used to wipe the cleaning liquid off windscreens. They were a problem and an accident waiting to happen. The police confiscated their buckets and squeezy bottles. At this time, we never had issues with people simply begging at traffic lights.

When this young woman came alongside my car window I politely shook my head and smiled. She wandered off with her paper cup to another car. I felt sad for her current situation and what she had become in life - a beggar.

The traffic lights changed to green and I moved on. I turned into the supermarket car park and found a car park space. I grabbed my heavy-duty shopping bags and made my way to the shop entrance. As usual, sitting on either side of the door were two beggars. This did not surprise me, as this was normal at almost every supermarket in Manchester. Two white males with paper cups and blankets. They did not speak so I ignored them. If they would have asked for money I would have politely refused. I never ignore someone begging. I always answer their request with a polite No. They are my fellow citizens and deserve an answer, for they are human. But they do not deserve my or your money.

I purchased my items. I gave myself a stiff talking to concerning the amount of alcohol purchased. I placed the bags of shopping in my car and walked around the corner to my favourite takeaway to get a kebab. I need to be honest with everyone here. If it was not for the convenience of this kebab shop then I may not be so dedicated to visiting my mum every week. I am just being honest. Please do not tell her.

I walked along the main road to reach my spicy destination. I walk past four white men begging outside four different shops. I recognised some faces as they are regulars in this location. This neighbourhood is predominately an Asian community. Yet I see no Asian beggars, only white ones.

Back to my car with my kebab and I headed home. I realised I needed fuel so popped into a garage to fill up. It is my usual garage on the outskirts of the city centre, it is always one of the cheapest for fuel. I also earn points on purchases which is a bonus. I drove into an empty space next to a petrol pump.

Almost immediately I was approached by a white man with a paper cup. "*Spare change, please.*" I politely shook my head and smiled. He walked away.

This was the first time I had been approached by a beggar while trying to fill my car with fuel. I had noticed that this petrol station had gained a few beggars sitting outside the kiosk entrance over the last year. The petrol station also had a cash point, so a beggar was always sitting there. On one occasion, I witnessed a beggar buying alcohol and then sitting back down outside to continue their trade. I mentioned the increase in this activity to the cashier as I paid for my fuel. She was apologetic. She explained that since the Covid lockdown fewer people were visiting the city centre, so beggars have found other places to beg. She also pointed out that a homeless hostel was only around the corner, so this location was convenient.

I drove the rest of the way home thinking about my experience that afternoon. Begging had become completely normalised and accepted. The general public did not seem to notice, or if they did, they did not care. Businesses accepted beggars as a new everyday problem that they were helpless to combat, so must be put up with.

I became angry as I drove home. Angry at the individuals who were too pathetic and weak to make a success of living in the UK. Angry at the police for not enforcing begging laws. Angry at the local government for allowing our fellow citizens to fall so low into despair.

Most of all, I was angry at society. Angry at the fools who think they are helping by handing over a few coins and sandwiches to people on the streets. Angry at people for not demanding action from the government. Where are the protests? Why does no one care about beggars, rough sleepers and the homeless?

I needed a spark to start the book, on a winter's Sunday afternoon I found it.

The spark was anger. Not necessarily at the individuals begging for they are broken individuals. But our willingness to help continue a negative lifestyle that damages the body and mind. A lifestyle that ruins lives.

A flurry of questions popped into my head. Do we not care? Do we see ourselves in the faces of beggars for we are also beggars? Do we envy those who have rejected their personal responsibility? Is there a difference between holding out a paper cup and receiving Universal Credit? Did the government's furlough scheme give us a taste of the life of a beggar? Or have we been going down this path for decades without ever noticing?

I started typing. I had a lot to say.

II. The Conversation

Before you jump into this book, allow me to explain my thoughts on street begging. I have two decades of hands-on experience with this topic. I previously chaired a multi-agency panel to seek solutions for individuals who were rough sleeping or begging. This panel consisted of the police, council, NHS, drug support services and other organisations. At the same time, I was responsible for reducing antisocial behaviour in Manchester city centre - this included begging, street drinking and rough sleeping. After I left the council, I set up charity projects that supported people off the streets and into accommodation. I also created a project that secured paid employment for homeless individuals. I have spoken at conferences and appeared on national media to discuss this topic. I am somewhat of an expert when it comes to rough sleeping and begging in Manchester.

Due to the above experience, people regularly asked me many questions on this topic. How should they help the dishevelled individuals they see sitting on street corners? I have answered every question you could possibly ask. I have debunked every excuse and every urban myth. I have looked into the eyes of wonderful individuals who just want to help their fellow man and told them they are part of the problem.

Allow me to share these questions and my answers with you in a form of a conversation for ease.

Instructions on how to help people

You see begging on a street corner: *Surely, it is a good thing to give a beggar a couple of coins?*

Unfortunately, the vast majority of beggars are drug addicts. A large proportion of these are not rough sleeping but have accommodation of some sort. How do we know? They tell us when we sit down with them to ask what help they need or want. The problem in Manchester is a mental health and drug problem. A few coins for more drugs is no solution.

I don't give money, I give them a sandwich, surely this can't be harmful?

No one is starving on the streets of Manchester. We have first-hand experience of rough sleepers telling us they don't need to attend a support centre that day for a meal - for they have already eaten on the street and have a bagful of sandwiches. Without accessing professional support vulnerable individuals cannot change their situation. Giving a meal-deal may make you feel better, but it does nothing for the individual sitting on the street.

I've heard that the homeless have to pay for rooms in a hostel?

Hostel costs are covered through Housing Benefits. Why would this not be the case? Hostel staff help individuals to claim the benefit once they have moved into the hostel.

Come on, people need a little help when they're down on their luck?

We completely agree, but doing the wrong thing for the right reasons doesn't help anyone. Supporting a drug habit doesn't help. Stopping someone from visiting a support centre doesn't help. Enabling someone to beg all day doesn't help. That's why staff work on the streets 5 days a week supporting people to access accommodation and support.

If we don't give them money, then won't they all just turn to crime?

Unfortunately, this is simply illogical. Should we give criminals money in the hope that they won't commit crime? Anyway, who said homeless people are criminals?

Be honest, you just want them off the streets because of the city's image?

We do not work for or receive any funding from the Council. We run our projects only for the benefit of vulnerable people in need. We do want them off the streets, but for their individual benefit and to protect their health.

Surely not everyone on the streets struggles with addiction?

Whilst we are not saying this, the point that we are trying to make is the link between begging and the misuse of hard drugs. Not between homelessness and begging or homelessness and drug misuse. So the question you need to ask yourself is why are you handing over money? You cannot presume it will help that person because from our experience it is having the opposite effect.

OK, you've convinced me. What should I do to help people get off the street and away from the dealers?

You should support a small local homeless charity that works frontline with people in need. These charities can get people into accommodation and employment. They also open bank accounts, arrange for passports for foreigners to get home, offer free hot meals, showers, internet, and phones. And let's not forget an important need we all have, an opportunity to socialise. To feel normal, to make friends, to talk and to have someone listen.

I am not asking you to just walk on by and ignore people who are begging or homeless. By all means, engage homeless people in conversation. Ask if you can help them, find out what help they need, and make referrals to support agencies. Or find the information yourself and hand it to them.

But please don't give money. Sadly, your kindness can kill and does!

Stories constitute the single
most powerful weapon in a leader's arsenal.

– Dr Howard Gardner

Chapter 1

The Beggar's Narrative

Every beggar has a story – a narrative. It is a complex mix of the truth, half-truths, make-believe, and pure lies. I should know, I have listened to hundreds.

Does this tangled mix of storytelling sound familiar? Of course it does. It is exactly what you do when telling a story. It is what I do. What we all do. We cherry-pick the best bits. We edit to make the story interesting, to reflect the person we wish we were, or the person someone else wants us to be. We ignore, forget and lie to create the best story possible. We reduce our responsibility for mistakes to alleviate embarrassment and fragility. Why would it be any different for a beggar? They are human and flawed just like us.

A narrative: a story or tale of a series of related events or experiences.

Storytelling is important to humans, it always has been. It is the way we pass down important information and knowledge. It is how we communicate. Over millennia, communities that did not embrace storytelling died out and their genes faded into history. People who knew the stories of where water could be found during a drought survived, as did the ones who remembered the stories of where food could be found at different times of the year. Tribes who created myths and legends to help guide individual behaviour benefited the community by reducing conflict. Children love stories for this is how they learn. My granddaughter has spent hours sitting on my knee listening to the adventures of ten little dinosaurs. At certain places in the book, we both loudly roar and annoy her mum. My grandad would tell me stories late at night in our shared bedroom of his exploits during WWII, this led me to travel the world to find my own stories.

Storytelling: the social and cultural activity of sharing stories.

We have been designed to see stories as valuable, this is why we read novels and watch films. This is how we pass down important information from one generation to another. We all have our favourite stories and they stay with us forever.

A lesson you learn very quickly when working with beggars is not to believe a word they say. I know this sounds harsh. You take everything with a pinch of salt and at face value. For there is nothing else you can do. You listen and act upon what they tell you, but you do not believe it until it has been confirmed or proven.

I learnt this lesson when my charity first started to work on the streets with rough sleepers. We met a man begging in the city centre, let's call him Jonesy. He was intelligent and affable. He told us he had been living on the streets for several years, sometimes accessing hostels when he was lucky. It was a hard life. He sometimes saved up the money he begged and used it to pay for a B&B or a space in an illegal squat for the night. We liked this man. It was obvious the system was failing him. Just the sort of person we wanted to help. The very reason we set up the project.

We asked if he wanted our help, he did. We made some notes of his circumstances and personal details. It took several weeks of chatting as he said he did not want to go into all the details in one session as it is upsetting. Plus, he was not convinced we could help – he had been promised many things from many people before. They all let him down. We promised we would help. He was grateful and thanked us. We were true to our word - we contacted the local council and other agencies. No one would speak to us about Jonesy for we did not have his written consent. Data protection and safeguarding policies kicked in. It took a month for us to satisfy partner agencies of who we were, that we had all the necessary policies and insurance. Eventually, the council agreed to speak to us. We explained who our client was, what he needed and why.

The council manager looked at us and nodded along as I spoke. When I finished he smiled and replied. He told us he personally knew the man in question. His smile disappeared as he began to tell us his version of Jonesy's situation and circumstance.

The council had known him for years. Many councils knew Jonesy. They had worked in partnership with another council to support Jonesy, for he travelled into the city centre on a daily basis from another area. He lived with his girlfriend in a council flat that was completely paid for through housing benefits. Jonesy and his girlfriend were on full benefits. They told us that Jonesy begged to fund his heroin habit. He had been an addict for over a decade and was known to every service offering support. He was not sleeping on the streets. In fact, according to their records, he had never slept on the streets, not even for one night.

We were shocked. We felt stupid. I could read the manager's face: *'another group of idiots who think they can walk around solving complicated problems.'* In hindsight, we were naïve. We wanted to believe Jonesy. We wanted to believe that the council were incompetent and uncaring. To be fair, I had worked for the council, I knew they were incompetent. But maybe my desire to believe my own bias was too strong to see through the lies. Maybe I just wanted to be a hero.

We clung to the only straw left available to us. The council were mistaken and had the wrong man in mind. This was a possibility. We all make mistakes. We needed to speak to Jonesy and clear up this mistake. Jones is a common surname.

A few days later we bumped into Jonesy. We sat down and told him about our meeting with the council and what they told us. His face slowly changed from smiling to deadpan. When we got to the end of the update we asked him if it was true. He slowly stood up. Picked up his bag and his begging sign. He turned to us and quietly told us to *'fuck off.'* He walked off slowly, as if without a care in the world. He was not aggressive or offended or embarrassed. The only description I can give is he looked inconvenienced.

I was again shocked. Part of me had hoped the council were

mistaken. That Jonesy would explain how there were a few Jonesy's on the streets and this mix-up had happened before. I had to give this incident a lot of thought. What had we done wrong? How could we make sure it did not happen again?

This was when I heard the term 'beggar's narrative' for the first time. I cannot remember who came up with it, or if I read it somewhere and adopted it. I would like to think I came up with the phrase, but I know I did not.

I realised to be a successful beggar you needed a story, a character, a role. It is acting. Plain and simple. This could be enhanced with props such as a cardboard sign, a dog or a sleeping bag. Begging is the ultimate in character acting – *Robert De Niro* would make a great beggar. You have to immerse yourself in the role. It is a performance that some of the general public pay to watch. The most talented rise to the top and earn the most money, just like in every profession. At some level, you have to totally believe what you are portraying is real.

Acting is an activity in which a story is told through its enactment by an actor who adopts a character. It involves a broad range of skills, including a well-developed imagination, emotional facility, physical expression, vocal projection, clarity of speech, and the ability to interpret drama.

Jonesy was good at acting, he was good at the game. He had his narrative perfected, crafted carefully over at least a decade. He told listeners that he was not a drug addict, for this helped them overcome the worry that any cash donated would not go straight to a drug dealer. He would slip into the conversation about how much B&Bs cost per night and that he nearly had that amount, just a few quid short. He would reminisce about living in a children's home and his exploits in the army, as this would help foster additional pity.

When asked about accepting the support on offer his answer would explain why he could not be helped. Homeless hostels would not accept him with his dog - we never saw him with a dog. The council could not help due to him being ex-military and not having roots in Manchester.

The British Legion could not help because he has lost all his identification so could not prove he was in the forces. The support centres are full of violence and drug dealers so he keeps away from them for safety.

He had an answer to everything you could possibly throw at him. He had been in the game a long time. He was experienced. He had a solid beggar's narrative. He was impressive.

But it was just a story. A mixture of the truth and lies. It had been created over a decade to bat away questions, solicit pity, and ultimately earn money.

We saw Jonesy dozens of times over the following years. He ignored us every time and never spoke to us again. His story was bust. He was defenceless. We were not worth speaking to for we offered no potential value or benefit. His Jedi mind trick did not work on people who knew it was just a trick. His beggar's narrative was a lie. He knew it, we knew it, he knew we knew it. An unofficial truce was implemented. He pretended he did not know us, and we pretended we had not been taken for a ride.

Begging For A Court-Martial

Army Joe was a character. Bright and intelligent. A pure victim of his own making. He was one of the only two veterans we ever worked with on the streets for they are rare. It is not true any longer that veterans are left to cope by themselves if they fall upon hard times. There is lots of help and support available, sometimes they do not take it, but it is there. Do not be fooled by a beggar telling you they are a veteran for in the vast majority of cases they are not. Army Joe was a veteran - a part of his narrative that was true.

Joe was physically a mess. Weeping ulcers on his legs that smelt of rotting flesh. His hands were bright red and swollen. But do not take his declining fitness as a sign of weakness - he was dangerous. You felt it in his presence, or at least I did. Amy Joe was not to be messed around, not without consequence.

He had an answer to any question you asked him. World politics. Climate change. Immigration. And of course, he had the answer to Manchester's rough sleeping crisis. He discussed how an unused police station on the outskirts of the city centre should be a one-stop-shop for rough sleepers. A hub containing the NHS, accommodation specialists, police, drug treatment, mental health services and support workers. A very good idea.

Joe had the fortune to meet the *Mayor of Greater Manchester*, Andy Burnham, one morning during a staged walkabout for the cameras to highlight what he was doing for rough sleepers. Burnham had made a campaign promise to eradicate rough sleeping in 3 years, as I write it has been 5 years. The numbers have gone down a little, but no eradication is in sight. Anyway, Joe gave him a piece of his mind. The Mayor contacted the council and later the same day their outreach team was speaking to Joe about a one-bedroom flat that was available. Amazing how a phone call from the Mayor can generate action if the Press are about.

Joe was given the flat. A great end to a sad story of a man that had served his country. But Joe was still sleeping on the streets in the city centre. I do not mean just begging, I mean sleeping. What went wrong?

I sat down next to Joe in St Anne's Square and asked what was going on. He explained. The flat was lovely. Just what he wanted. But he had two problems. The previous tenant's belongings were still in the flat and took up major parts of the living room and bedroom. He did not want to throw the stuff out for he knew what it felt like to lose all your possessions. The previous tenant was now in jail. The second problem was that the flat had no gas or electricity. Both utility meters were broken. He stayed one night, sat in the dark, could not even make a cup of tea, or wash in hot water. What was the point in remaining? He left for the streets.

I asked him if he had reported the issues to his council support worker? He confirmed he had. The council constantly surprise me with their level of incompetence and inaction. It had been nine months since he was given the flat. I asked if he wanted me to speak to the council. He did.

I emailed the council and hit a brick wall. They could not speak to me unless I sent a signed consent form from Joe. I sent one. I then had to chase for a response. After four weeks I got a meeting with a manager. We discussed Joe.

His flat was a privately owned property with the rent guaranteed by the council. They knew about all of Joe's complaints, their answer to why none of them had been fixed was the same - Joe was difficult. Yes, he was. Most rough sleepers are difficult. But they had placed him in the accommodation and should take some responsibility for it. Where was the customer service for their service user?

They also told me that Joe was being very naughty. He was receiving housing benefits for his flat directly into his bank account every month but was spending it on heroin. The landlord did not care for the rent was guaranteed by the council if not paid.

I suggested that I would be the conduit between Joe and the council. Together we would get Joe's flat sorted so he moves back in.

I arranged for a sit down meeting in the middle of St Anne's Square for me, Joe and his council support officer. We all agreed on a plan and a way forward. By the time I got back to my office the plan had been vetoed by a council manager. I gave up. This was the end of my project working on the streets with rough sleepers. I had no more energy. You cannot beat the system, you have to work within it. Only someone like the Mayor can change it and even he would struggle. We changed the aim of our project so we did not have to rely on the council and started to help former rough sleepers into employment.

If I had managed to get the council to do their job would Joe have stayed in the flat? No. I do not think he would have. He was addicted to the streets. He was a somebody on the streets. All the council did was give him a solid gold excuse to sleep rough and validate his victimhood status. Plus, a waste of a one-bedroom flat that someone else in need could have benefited from.

The streets were very appealing to Joe. Free food was brought to him by strangers. An extra £500 per month was placed into his bank account every month from housing benefits. This is on top of his Universal Credit and disability allowance payments. He would top up these State payments with his role as a local 'spice dealer.' An illegal synthetic drug preferred by street people for it is powerful and cheap. All in all, he was probably earning more money per month than many full-time employees. What did he do with his income? The track lines that covered his body should give us a clue.

Begging is the practice of imploring others to grant a favour or a gift of money, with little or no expectation of repayment. A person doing such is called a beggar. Beggars may operate in public places such as transport routes, urban parks, and markets. Besides money, they may also ask for food, drinks, cigarettes or other small items.

Definitions of begging include:

- asking for food or money as charity
- asking someone earnestly or humbly for something.
- imploring others to grant a favour with no expectation of reciprocation

Begging is illegal in England & Wales under the 1824 *Vagrancy Act* and carries a sentence of up to one month's hard labour. This law is still used today to tackle begging. It is fair to say that this law is extremely out of date and ineffective, not surprising for a 200-year-old piece of legislation.

The *Vagrancy Act 1824* is an Act of Parliament of the United Kingdom that makes it an arrestable offence to sleep rough or beg. I do not know of a single case where someone has been arrested for sleeping rough; it is only used to combat begging, if ever used.

The law was enacted to deal with the increasing numbers of homeless poor in England and Wales following the end of the Napoleonic Wars in 1815. Nine years after the Battle of Waterloo the British Army and British Navy had undergone a massive reduction in size, leaving large numbers of discharged military personnel without jobs or accommodation. Many were living rough on the streets. At the same time, a massive influx of economic migrants from Ireland and Scotland arrived in England, especially London, in search of work. Politicians became concerned that the police were becoming ineffective in controlling vagrancy.

The majority of the original *Vagrancy Act 1824* remains in force in England and Wales currently, although it is currently being repealed. In 1982 the entire Act was repealed in Scotland. Part of the Act has been repealed in Northern Ireland.

Begging For Christmas

A few years ago in early December, we helped a young man off the streets and into a homeless hostel. A place had come up unexpectedly. He was very lucky. It was truly a Christmas miracle!

We visited him several times to make sure things were going OK. Getting individuals into accommodation was the easy bit, making sure they stayed in the accommodation was the tricky part. Some people get bored and walk out, others are pulled back to the streets for drugs, and some are kicked out for intolerable behaviour. His support worker told us he was doing fine.

During one visit we noticed he was sitting at the kitchen table with another resident of the hostel. They seemed to be involved in an arts & crafts session. The first I ever heard about these types of sessions for homeless people I laughed and thought they were 'pink and fluffy' nonsense. A waste of time and money. I was completely wrong. They are therapeutic and a form of mental health therapy. A way of expressing yourself without the need for communication skills. An opportunity to create a piece of art that you keep, that you can hang on a wall and be proud of.

If you have failed in life, you feel insignificant and worthless. You are nothing. But if you can create something beautiful, something unique then you realise you must have talent within you. Beauty cannot be created out of nothing. Pride makes you hang it on the wall for others to see. It is a statement of your existence for you are not invisible. And in most cases, it becomes a possession that has meaning – which is important when you have lost every other personal trinket.

We walked over to the kitchen table to offer some encouragement and praise their creativity. It was not what we had expected. They were being artistic and very creative, just not in a way we could encourage. They were making festive begging signs.

Large pieces of cardboard contained the usual message: 'I am homeless – please help!.' They had decorated the signs with colourful drawings of Christmas images, such as Santa, holly leaves and wrapped presents. The piste de résistance was the battery-powered Christmas fairy lights inserted along the edge of the cardboard sign. The fairy lights were £1.99 from a local shop. Bargain.

It was obvious that they had spent a lot of time on the project. They looked amazing, the most impactful signs we had ever seen. They were both pleased with their work. I would say they were proud, it showed on their faces. They had never spent such an amount of time before on something creative. They both actively showed us their signs. It was like a child coming home from school with a new painting, they were super excited and beaming.

We smiled. Told them that the signs looked great. But then we had to bring them back to reality. We reminded them that they were not homeless anymore. The signs were a lie. They were liars.

The money earned from begging was the reason why they both had ended up on the streets in the first place. And if they were not careful, the money earned from these signs would put them right back where we had found them.

Their heads went down. No more conversation. No more eye contact. We were dismissed. They had the same look on their faces as Jonesy had when we blew his beggar's narrative out of the water by accident. A good beggar's narrative only works if you can set aside reality and immerse yourself in the fiction – a lie is not a lie if you believe it to be true. Both men had spent so long making the signs that they had slipped into their begging roles and had been rudely brought back to reality.

We spoke to their support worker about our concern. She had no concern. Her take on the matter was that making the signs kept them quiet and 'art' was good therapy. What they do outside of the 'home' is not her concern. Her job was to ensure a peaceful shift.

This lack of a holistic approach is why so many rough sleepers end up back on the streets so quickly. We set them up to fail. We allow them, sometimes even encourage them, to make poor choices that continue their decline into hell. An agency will tackle a little bit of the issue, the bit they get paid to do. The rest is left to someone else to figure out.

Begging To Be Conned

Begging is not just the act of sitting on a cold pavement with a paper cup. Begging is complicated. It changes over time to take advantage of new customers, new environments and new technologies. When times change, a new approach may be needed to separate fools from their hard-earned money.

Online begging is big business. Just look at sites like *JustGiving* and *GoFundMe*. They are simply begging sites - but not all begging is immoral. When the complete truth is told and people still decide to help a cause, then this is a free choice based on correct information. I am all for free choice and personal responsibility. I only have an issue when lies are told to pull at heartstrings to obtain money under false pretences. If someone was sitting on a wet pavement with a sign asking for money to buy crack cocaine then anyone who donates would know exactly where the money was going. They could make an informed choice to give or not. My issue is when the beggar's narrative is a lie.

A friend of a friend of a friend told me this story. I believe it to be true. A family's pet dog was sick and needed an operation costing thousands. The kids were upset. The father set up a 'save the family pet' donation page to raise the funds needed. (I have issues with spending huge amounts of money on vets – my wife tells me that sometimes I am not a nice person.) The online page did very well and over £3000 was raised. The dog was now saved. An honest donation page that raised money from dog lovers to save the life of a dog. What could be wrong with that?

While raising the money to save the dog, a friend offered them some advice and a solution. They knew of a local vet that was subsidised by animal charities and private donations. They offered huge discounts to animal owners on State Benefits. The family were not on benefits but their friend who offered the advice was and offered to take the dog to the vet. The dog visited the vet and its life was saved. The bill came to less than £100. Amazing. Now, what became of the £3000 I can hear you asking? Was it donated to charity or to the vet who saved their dog's life? No. A family holiday was booked and paid for upfront.

This fraudulent use of the money was not the initial intention of the fundraising page. The dog did receive the treatment required. But the act of begging erodes our sense of morality. You do not see the people who donate as kind people, but rather as fools with excess money. You play mental gymnastics to convince yourself that keeping the money is acceptable and victimless. You know better. But you play along with your narrative for you are greedy, selfish and immoral. We all are.

A modern twist on a very old beggar's narrative is the *lonely hearts* scam. Begging only works when you can influence how someone feels. Feelings are very important, they control many of our decisions without us even realising. A beggar who generates feelings of disgust, anger or fear does not earn. A good beggar generates feelings such as shame, pity or guilt. They also trigger positive emotions after you have given, sometimes with words of praise. *God bless you! You are a saint!* Begging is always about the 'giver,' never the beggar.

In a world where we are living much longer and 42% of marriages end in divorce, many fairly well off people are seeking love again. Combine this with online dating and we have a hunting ground for beggars with credible narratives. These people exist and earn a good living.

The beggar builds up a relationship with a lonely person online. Time is spent cultivating a relationship and trust. The lonely person feels special, desired, and wanted. They feed off the compliments and crave more validation. A problem occurs. The compliments may stop because the beggar has a problem that only money can solve. It is not a lot of money. The money is dropped into the paper cup so the affection can continue. The good feelings continue. Another issue arrives. More money is electronically donated. Another issue arrives. A lot more money is needed this time. Paying for issues to go away has worked well up to now. Why would it not continue?

We may look upon this as a scam and think it has nothing to do with begging. But begging mostly is a scam. Asking for money by pulling on someone's heartstrings is begging and it is also a scam. But looking at it as only a scam does not help potential victims from spotting the scam when played upon them.

The scam is not the taking of the money for this is freely given. The giver gets positive emotional feelings in return for helping and donating. You could say these emotions are paid for. The scam is the falsehood of the relationship. This is what hurts the victim when the scam is revealed not the financial loss, for this was given freely.

A Fool And His Money Are Soon Parted.
– Thomas Tusser

A confidence trick is an attempt to defraud a person or group after first gaining their trust. Confidence tricks exploit victims using their credulity, compassion, vanity, irresponsibility, and greed. They can also be known as a con game, a con, a scam, a grift, a hustle, a bunko, a swindle, a flimflam, a gaffle, or a bamboozle. The intended victims are known as marks, suckers, stooges, mugs, rubes, or gulls (from the word gullible). When accomplices are employed, they are known as shills. Confidence tricks exploit typical human characteristics such as greed, dishonesty, opportunism, lust, credulity, irresponsibility, desperation, and naïvety.

A 'short con' or 'small con' is a fast swindle that can take just minutes. A 'long con' or 'big con' or 'long game' is a scam that unfolds over several days or weeks. It may involve a team, props, sets, extras, costumes, and scripted lines. It aims to rob the victim of huge sums of money or valuables, often by getting them to empty banking accounts or borrow from family members.

In '*Confessions of a Confidence Man*,' Edward H. Smith lists six steps or stages of a confidence game.

1. Foundation work: preparations are made in advance of the game and studying the background knowledge needed for the role.

2. Approach: the victim is approached or contacted.

3. Build-up: the victim is allowed to profit from participating in a scheme. The victim's greed is encouraged, such that their rational judgment of the situation might be impaired.

4. Pay-off or convincer: the victim receives a small payout as a demonstration of the scheme's purported effectiveness. This may be a real amount of money or faked in some way. In a gambling con, the victim is allowed to win several small bets. In a stock market con, the victim is given fake dividends.

5. The 'hurrah': a sudden manufactured crisis or change of events forces the victim to act or make a decision immediately. This is the point at which the con succeeds or fails. With a financial scam, the con artist may tell the victim that the 'window of opportunity' to make a large investment in the scheme is about to suddenly close forever.

6. The in-and-in: a conspirator (in on the con, but assumes the role of an interested bystander) puts an amount of money into the same scheme as the victim, to add an appearance of legitimacy. This can reassure the victim, and give the con man greater control when the deal has been completed.

Cons succeed by inducing judgment errors in the victim. A con usually exploits character flaws such as 'dishonesty,' 'greed,' and 'gullibility.' I remember dealing with many students in the city centre who would complain to the police about being robbed by drug dealers while trying to purchase illegal drugs. They would walk down a dark side street to do the deal, pull out their money, and walk back unhappy with no drugs.

As a society, we try to educate against these flaws through the use of popular sayings: '*no such thing as a free lunch*,' '*you don't get something for nothing,' 'too good to be true,' 'fools and their money are easily parted.'*

Sometimes you cannot help someone who is being conned for the need to believe in the opportunity is greater than their sense of reality. A friend of mine tells this story of when she worked in a high street bank.

A customer came in and wanted to transfer a very large amount of his savings into his everyday current account. Bank protocols kicked in. My friend politely enquired about the reason for such a transfer, as she was completing the necessary transfer forms. This was over a decade ago and banks were fully aware of such scams - this was before the onslaught of emails claiming to be your bank.

The customer stated that he had inherited a small fortune in Hong Kong and needed some money to pay solicitor fees, government taxes and a license fee. Fifteen thousand pounds would be a small price to pay to get his hands on approximately half a million.

My friend stopped typing. It was an obvious con. Even without her fraud training, she would have known it was a scam. But not everyone is the same. She told him what she thought. He disagreed and pulled out a printout of the email explaining everything.

She read the printout and googled the company name. A list of articles appeared all discussing this scam. How it was the latest in a series of similar scams, and detailed some of the people who had fallen for it. She spun the computer screen for the customer to read. He did.

He was not convinced. He referred back to the printout he held and explained that he was going to get half a million. My friend alerted her manager of the situation for she was extremely concerned. The manager explained everything again to the customer but he was still adamant.

Finally, the manager instructed my friend to complete the transaction. Everything had been done by the bank to protect their customer. The money belonged to the customer and he was entitled to transfer it to his current account. He did. We do not know what happened after that.

Begging For Charity

Charities are beggars. I should know, I founded a multi-award-winning one and still support it. I have begged for money, free office space, accountants, legal advice, stationery, laptops and even gym equipment. It was all legitimate. But it was all begging nonetheless. I do not wish to sound big-headed, but I am a bloody good beggar. Why? Because I had a great narrative and storytelling ability.

Charities are excellent beggars. It is their *raison d'être*. The big ones have mastered the art of formulating a beggar's narrative and selling it to the masses. They have swapped the traditional cardboard sign for our television and smartphone. They do not need £1.99 fairy lights to grab your attention for they have marketing teams to create the most heartfelt videos you can possibly imagine. The starving African children with swollen bellies, large eyes and wearing rags. A young girl stares into the camera as the narrator tells the story of her sexual abuse. We have all seen these videos, they are picture-perfect in terms of a beggar's narrative.

They are not designed to pull on your heartstrings - they are designed to rip it out and rent it back to you. You must pay if you want internal peace. They are not interested in a few coins as a one-off donation, they want to hook you for life. This is how they maximise their return on investment by securing regular giving by direct debit. Many charities also want you to pay even when you have left this earthly pleasure. They help you to leave a legacy donation by arranging for the necessary legal paperwork to be drafted, signed and recorded. There is nothing innately wrong with any of this for they are truthful about where they will spend your money. But there are some valid questions about tactics and methods.

Some of the less savoury tactics can be classed as *Poverty Porn:* any type of media, be it written, photographed or filmed, which exploits the dire situation of highlighted people to generate increased charitable donations or support for a given cause. It also suggests that the viewer of the exploited is motivated by the gratification of base instincts. It can also be used for films that objectify people in poverty for the sake of entertaining a privileged audience.

The concept of poverty porn was first introduced in the 1980s. Charity campaigns made use of hard-hitting images such as pictures of malnourished children with flies in their eyes. Some of these campaigns were successful in raising a lot of money for charities. Critics claimed it oversimplified chronic poverty. Large charities use graphic depictions of famine, poverty, war and especially children to attract sympathy and increase donations.

The rise in popularity of reality TV shows has leant towards poverty porn. Shows like *Jeremy Kyle, Super Scroungers* and *Benefits Street* were designed to exploit a specific section of the 'poor' purely for entertainment value.

Begging For Fairtrade

Fairtrade is an arrangement to help producers in poorer countries get a better price for their produce by meeting a series of expectations, such as paying better wages and looking after the environment. It applies to many commodities, especially chocolate and coffee. A logo on the product advertises that it is produced under Fairtrade regulations.

Fairtrade purchases are growing in the UK, as shoppers equate the logo with better pay for poor farmworkers. An ethical way to give to poor countries? Or like many donations in the UK, is it just guilt money?

One 2015 study published by the *MIT Press* concluded that producer benefits were close to zero because there was an oversupply of Fairtrade certification. On average, producers sell 18% to 37% of their output as Fairtrade certified. It is argued that the financial benefit is just enough to pay the costs of certification.

Evidence suggests that little of the extra money paid by consumers actually reaches the farmers. One British café chain was passing less than one per cent of the extra charge incurred by customers to the exporting cooperative. The Finish pay considerably more for Fairtrade certified coffee, but only 11.5% of the extra paid goes to the exporting country. US Fairtrade coffee costs $5 per lb extra at retail, of which the exporting cooperative receives 2% to 10%.

Fairtrade is profitable for traders in richer countries and richer farmers. The majority of Fairtrade suppliers are in the higher income or middle income developing countries, such as Costa Rica and Mexico, with relatively few in the poorest countries.

Where you have money to be made, you have corruption. Labourers on Fairtrade farms in Peru have been paid less than the minimum wage. In 2006, a *Financial Times* journalist found that all ten mills they visited sold uncertified coffee as certified Fairtrade.

A good 'con' needs a good narrative. Most people do not care if the poor are helped, they just want not to feel guilty that they have a better life because of a freak of nature – meaning they were born in the UK.

Begging The Issue

The Big Issue is a UK street newspaper founded in September 1991 and now published in four continents. It exists to offer homeless people, or individuals at risk of homelessness, the opportunity to earn a legitimate income, thereby helping them to reintegrate into mainstream society. It is the world's most widely circulated street newspaper.

To become a vendor, one must be homeless or almost homeless, vulnerably housed or marginalised in some way. Basically, anyone can sell it. It has nothing to do with rough sleeping, yet the vast majority of the general public thinks it has.

Big Issue North is a Manchester version launched in December 1992 to cover the North of England. This is the only publication I have worked with, witnessed on the streets, and spoken to their vendors and staff. I have never bought the magazine and regularly convince others not to. Why?

The Big Issue is a con. It may not have started that way, but for the last fifteen years, while I have been aware of it, it has been. It is successful because it has a great narrative – buy a magazine and help someone off the street. A simple message – but a complete load of rubbish for many reasons.

The magazine has nothing to do with rough sleeping. I am not aware of one single person who was rough sleeping to ever sell it, not one. Individuals who are sleeping on the streets are in no state of mind to sell magazines. They cannot collect money, save half of it to purchase new copies the next day. These damaged individuals cannot see past the next few hours and are only concerned about where their need fix is coming from.

The magazine is legalised begging on a corporate scale. If the vendors are not sleeping on the streets, then who are they? They fall within two groups. Eastern Europeans have replaced traditional begging with this new form of respectable begging which is officially classed as a job. The other group are functioning drug addicts who use the money they earn to subsidise their drug habit. Of course, the odd exception can be found and highlighted when the uncomfortable truth is discussed. I am not the only person within the homeless sector to feel this way about the magazine. Many do.

I watched a video a few years ago produced by *The Big Issue* showcasing their work and vendors. One vendor was talking about how *The Big Issue* is wonderful and explained why he sells it. If my memory serves me correctly, he was working on a building site but did not like the hours so decided to start to sell the magazine instead. He now has a better quality of life and earns more money. What sort of project enables individuals in full-time employment to quit their job and become a beggar on the streets selling a magazine? The answer is clear – a project that makes a profit from the sale of magazines. *The Big Issue* is only about sales and profit. I have spoken to former staff who say exactly the same thing.

If it was about moving people into a better life, then why are the same vendors working on the streets of Manchester for decades? I know one man who sells the magazine on a particular street in the city centre. He has been there for at least 15 years which I know of. He is a well-known heroin addict and so emaciated that a gush of wind could knock him over. Why is he still standing on a street corner? Why can he not be helped with a better job? Why is he trapped selling a rag to fund his habit?

There are many stated rules you have to follow to sell the magazine, but of course, they are all ignored and not enforced for this affects sales and profits. It is the Wild West on the streets once you put on your branded hi-vis waistcoat. Many vendors openly beg for money. Ask for more than the stated magazine price, and even encourage customers not to take the magazine so they can sell it again. Some vendors sell their branded waistcoats and lanyard to non-vendors for a profit and report them lost or stolen to the office for a replacement.

I remember in my old council job trying to deal with a non-official vendor who had purchased a hi-vis waistcoat to look the part but was engaged in fraud. His scam was to buy one real magazine from a vendor and place it on top of a handful of free magazines from local shops or the free supplements in newspapers. Like a card cheat, he would deal from the bottom of the deck when he made a sale. He would take a free magazine, roll it up, and kindly place it in the customer's shopping bag. The magazine would not be opened until they reached home. We got a few complaints but no one wanted to put in an official statement.

Another memorable incident was a Roma family who sold the magazine outside a sandwich shop targeting lunchtime workers. They took it in shifts to work and all sat in a wheelchair when outside the shop. At the change of shift, they jumped up to allow their relative to sit down and continue the con. Props are important, that is why many have dogs.

The huge flaw with street magazines is they keep people on the streets. This is the last place we want them to be. They socialise with other broken individuals, have easy access to drugs, are preyed upon by evil individuals, and continue their chaotic lifestyle. We need to move people off the streets and into decent productive lives with jobs. Our bigotry of low expectations allows them to continue their cycle of self-damage.

We tell them *The Big Issue* is a real job, they know they are beggars.

Begging Animals

Some animals beg. If you have a pet dog you know this to be true. Just like humans, animals beg for food mostly, but also to play and to be groomed. Birds have been studied the most in relation to begging.

In 1950, Tinbergen and Perdeck tested the effects of visual stimuli on begging behaviour by gull chicks. They used models emphasising different characteristics of the parent's bills to see what triggered the begging for food. These studies showed the chicks responded to the red spot on their parents' bill. This was not learnt behaviour but instinct.

Birds use begging calls to get attention from their parents to be fed. There is no point in begging if no one knows what you are doing, you must advertise the fact. But chicks giving repeated begging calls advertise their position to predators. This has been tested by comparing plundering rates of artificial nests with and without audio playbacks of bird begging calls. Nests with begging calls were destroyed sooner than 'quiet' nests. There is a downside to begging.

Atlantic Canary chicks display brightly coloured mouths as they beg for food from their parents. The intensity of the colour changes to reflect the hunger need of the bird, parents notice this and offer chicks food accordingly. In controlled experiments with two chicks, one of whom had its mouth artificially reddened with food colouring, parents constantly gave this chick more food. Visual stimuli enhance the success of begging.

Captive animals held in zoos or wildlife parks will often perform begging behaviour for food from staff and members of the public. In a study of Oriental Small-Clawed Otters it was found that when begging from visitors to the zoo, they only begged from those wearing blue shirts like that worn by the keepers. They learnt that blue shirts mean more food.

Studies have shown that the endocrine system (network of glands that produce hormones) could be a regulating system for begging behaviour. Elevated levels of testosterone are correlated with more intense and longer begging displays in birds. Is testosterone the reason why the vast majority of beggars on the streets are men? Interesting.

Begging For A Good Narrative

There are two distinct aspects to a good narrative. Both must be present when begging, but they do not have to be in equal measure. One can partly compensate for the other to a certain extent, but both must exist.

The first is appearance - we are visual creatures. We have excellent eyesight compared to other animals, except birds of prey. We experience the world through vision. We are constantly trying to improve our world by changing what we see. We create art. We paint our homes. We spend money on fashion. Let us not forget make-up, gardens, photographs, painted fingernails, the shape of our car and even how our hair is styled. All chefs understand that a good meal begins when we gaze upon the plate – we take the first bite with our eyes. *That looks tasty! I don't like the look of that!*

The second is emotional - we are emotional creatures. We have large complicated brains that were designed for us to live in social groups. We have to balance the need for what is good for us, against what is good for the group. We develop emotional connections with places, people and items. We cry at sad films even though we know it is not real. We miss particular aspects of our home when we are away on holiday. We welcome strangers into our family if they make another family member happy. We welcome animals as family pets. How many times have you done or said something stupid because you were emotional? *I'm never speaking to that person again! Let's be best friends forever!*

Appearance - a beggar has to look the part. They have to pass the eyesight test. This is not a conscious investigation, it happens automatically as your eyes seek as much information as possible. A person has to look like what they are portraying themselves to be or your brain notices the contradiction and issues a warning. If you are a street beggar then you need to look in distress, dirty, hungry and in immediate need of assistance. This can be aided with the use of props that subconsciously validate any initial assessment of the situation. A sleeping bag and rucksack imply you are sleeping on the streets without a word being said. A dog next to you implies you are a caring person. Old and dirty clothes signal that you are not able to look after yourself and are in urgent need.

A beggar sat on a street corner in new clean clothes, clean-shaven, with no props and using his iPhone will not generate any donations. This picture is all wrong. He may be in desperate need. He may have just been kicked out of his home or released from jail and will be sleeping on the streets that evening. He does not have a sleeping bag as a prop because he does to even have a sleeping bag. None of this matters. If you do not visually portray what you are, or want to be seen as then you do not pass the eye test in terms of a beggar's narrative.

Other types of beggars will use different types of visual methodology to pass the eye test. The family with the poorly dog would have posted pictures of the dog playing with their children and maybe one of the dog with big eyes looking into the camera. The charity videos will feature African kids where you can see their ribs through a lack of food. The sexually abused girl will be pretty with big eyes staring through the lens and into your soul. The lonely hearts scam will have photos of a fairly good looking person as the fake avatar. Some photos will have them doing normal things like being on holiday or spending time with their children. Once we visually see a person we automatically start to create our own impression of them based on these images, aka first impressions.

We see more than we think we see. I worked with a lovely lady who thought she was physic. She recounted a story of her husband parking the car during a long journey so he could have a rest and the children could have the lunch she had packed. She was not happy where he had parked initially and made him move 100 meters – the spot did not feel right to her. As they were eating their homemade sandwiches, a speeding car spun off the road and crashed into a tree right where they had previously parked. This car would have ploughed into their car if they had not moved. She obviously put this piece of good luck down to her new gift of foretelling the future. What else could it have been?

I asked some questions. Was she protective of her children? Was she extra cautious when her children were in a car? Was where they parked on a bend in the road? Did she notice speeding cars on the road? Had it been raining? She answered YES to all questions.

I explained that she did not have a special gift but that she was in 'mum mode' looking out for potential danger. She had subconsciously noticed the poor driving conditions that day. That the initial parking spot was on a bend in the road, and that the trajectory of a car that lost control would be close to their car. She saw it all without ever realising she was even looking.

Emotional - this is where we separate the average beggar from the exceptional. Understanding the emotional levers that operate within the subconscious of a person is deep, but to have the ability to manipulate these levers takes training and skill. Like many life skills, if you practise you get better. But there are always some people who are just naturally gifted in any particular field. This is also true in the field of soliciting an emotional response. This is why a small group of Hollywood actors are paid so well and appear in the biggest films – they do something to us emotionally.

A street beggar taps into a person's emotions by having a sad story that answers obvious questions before they are even asked. Questions such as how did you end up in this situation? Why are you not receiving help and support? Why are you sleeping on the street?

A beggar does not want to get into the nitty-gritty of their situation – they just want your money. Plain and simple. They may also want to get off the streets, not have a drug habit, make contact with their family and ultimately have a better life. All this may be true and usually is. But at the moment you are talking to them, you are just a potential ATM.

A good story will involve childhood trauma or abuse for we all have a high disgust response to the plight of children. Someone has to be mentioned as the villain in the story – without a villain, there is no one to blame. The best candidate will be someone we all know and have had negative dealings with, usually *The State*.

Council services let them down and failed them. They allowed them to be abused as a child or did not offer mental health services when they were in need. Or took away their kids based on lies, or evicted them for no good reason. They were let down by the system, victimised by the very people paid to protect them. We can all relate to the incompetence, red-tape and bureaucracy of a council.

They cannot get the help they need not because they do not want it, but because of issues or barriers placed in their way. *All the hostels are full. Foreigners get help first not British people. They have lost their ID so services cannot help. They are not entitled to help because they are ex-forces or not originally from that area. Accepting help means giving up their dog who is their best friend. They are too afraid of visiting support centres because of the violence and drug dealing. Or even, they are banned from accessing services for a crime they did not commit.* There are a million more reasons but these are the most common in my experience.

A good story needs more than clear pre-emptive answers, it needs emotion. It needs those little bits that flesh out a good story with character development. You have to be made to care about the character. This is achieved by interconnecting positive traits to yourself in the story - things we look up to and admire. But due to no fault of your own, these traits backfired and led to a poor outcome. I have heard the following lines many times: *I would rather sleep on the streets than give my dog up - he loves me. My mum said I was a problem for her, so I left so she could be happy. I could not take the abuse any longer so I ran away from home and cannot go back. My wife died of cancer and my life just fell apart.*

Other types of beggars will use different types of oral methodology to generate an emotional response. The man with the poorly dog talked about how the children will be so upset if the dog dies because it is part of the family. They gave a story of how their dog saved one of the children from a dog attack. A charity will explain how a small amount of money can go a long way and even save a life - £2.50 will feed a child for a week - £1 will vaccinate a child against a disease for life. The lonely hearts scam talks about being on their own and wanting to share their life, or how their last partner cheated on them and hurt them deeply. All these narratives impart positive character traits. Things you have been told to seek out, admire and desire. We take things at face value for we are social creatures who trust others. Sometimes it is easy to believe falsehoods if you want them to be true – just ask my friend the banker!

Dwell not on the faults and shortcomings
of others; instead, seek clarity about your own.

- Buddha

Chapter 2

A recovering beggar

If I am to explore what it takes to 'make a beggar,' then I will probably stumble over many aspects of this topic. Some of my thoughts may come across as controversial, uncaring and potentially upsetting. I will be quite critical as we go along, I will not hold back my punches. For this reason, I think it is best if I look at myself first in terms of my character, flaws and history. One cannot explore such a topic without delving into one's own personal experience. I will start by laying bare myself, warts and all. So that later, I may be seen as speaking from a position of knowledge, rather than a hypocrite.

"Hello everyone, my name is Nick, and I am a beggar."

This is how members at *Alcoholics Anonymous* introduce themselves at every meeting, so I thought I would copy the format. There are parallels between begging and alcohol dependency. The use of alcohol by people sitting on the street begging used to be commonplace, but it has dramatically reduced over decades due to the low cost of illegal drugs. These are easier to access and have a much greater effect on consciousness. Alcohol is not the drug of choice anymore for most broken people on the streets.

The above *Alcoholics Anonymous* statement is helpful physiologically, it allows you to admit to yourself your shortcomings so that a remedy can be sought. You cannot solve a problem until you admit you have a problem. Hence why all meetings begin with an admission of a problem.

Have I ever sat on the pavement with a paper cup in my hand and a sad look on my face? No. But there are different forms of begging, just as there many types of beggars. I want this book to explore the many types of begging we have in the UK and try to find explanations on why begging is seen as a valid option to gain what you want.

I shall begin my story. I was born a beggar, like everyone else in the world. We all are born knowing only how to beg. We beg for food, for warmth and attention. Infant mammals are nature's most prolific beggars. If they did not beg they would die. It is a natural survival instinct. Adults are predisposed to react to this type of behaviour from babies and children. It is a symbiotic relationship. A giver and a taker. The taker gets what it needs, and the giver gets a reward of positive emotion. The instinct of being a giver is so ingrained within women that new mothers can start to lactate upon hearing their baby cry. It does not even have to be their baby, other babies crying can have the same effect. A cat meowing can also trigger this reaction – as my auntie can verify. The sound of a baby in need triggers a biological response – this is hardwired into us at a very deep level.

My parents split up when I was 2 years old. I never saw my father again, he died when I was 6 years old. I have no memory of him. We moved in with my grandparents and lived with them until they both eventually died. As a child, I knew we received money from the State, it was called *Income Support*. I knew this meant my mum was not allowed to work. Working was not permitted if you had your hand out to the State. That was the deal. We give you money, and you stay dependent upon us forever. I do not know if any of my friends' parents were claiming State handouts, they all had at least one working parent. They all also had 2 parents in the home.

It was during the transition into secondary school that I first noticed where my family's income originated compared to my friends. My mum was given a council voucher to buy me a new school uniform. We went to a shop in the city centre that would accept the voucher. None of my friends visited this shop. No complaints. It was a nice shop as far as I can remember.

On the first day at my new school, I had to queue up at the admin office to receive 5 free dinner tickets for that week. I had been on free school dinners all the way through primary school but had never needed a dinner ticket before. None of my friends was in the weekly queue. I received free school meals until I was 18 years old and completed my A-levels at sixth form college.

Going to college was easy. There was no pressure for me to get a job - *Income Support* subsidised me until I was 18 years old. College was preferred by some parents for their child. It was better than them dropping in and out of employment and being a financial liability to the family. Safer to be guaranteed a State handout. I do not think this was the case for me, for a more accurate answer you will need to ask my mum. But it was the reason for a family member as I remember the conversation around the kitchen table.

After college, I drifted, as I looked for my role in life for I was lost. I looked for a long time. I signed on the dole dozens of times. I work some crappy jobs, some while signing on. I went travelling around the world. I became self-employed and still signed on whenever I needed extra. I usually signed off mainly to get the Jobcentre off my back after 6 months of claiming. I would leave it a week or two and sign on again for up to another six months. I wasted a decade of my life and was paid poorly to do so.

Over this time, I took advantage of many free government schemes and initiatives. They were purportedly designed to help the unemployed gain employment or improve their lives. I claimed a free eco-friendly fridge freezer. I had my savings doubled several times by the government for joining a savings club. I got my home insulated for free. I received a reconditioned computer for free. I got two free new suits and shirts to attend job interviews. I attended free evening classes to learn French. I nearly went on a scuba diving instructor training course paid for by the Jobcentre. But changed my mind due to it being winter, I am such a moaner when it comes to being cold. Everything was free. I expected it to be free.

To try to be fair to the government, I did access a few schemes that were helpful. The first was a self-employment course that helped me set up as a market trader and secure two grants to buy stock and a van. The other was a scheme to help poor people buy a house by offering a grant. With this grant on offer and my savings, I purchased my first house for cash. It had been vacant for years, it took me 3 years to fix up while living in the mess of a building site. I still do not know why it was a government policy to give me a grant to be a homeowner?

Much of the above did not help me as an unemployed person in seeking work – most of it was a waste of money. I was just a tick in a box to say an unemployed person had been given help. It fostered within me a dependency on handouts. And most surprisingly, it created fear. Fear of what handouts I would lose if I accept my responsibility and got a proper job. The good intentions of out of touch governments contributed to my feeling of being trapped within a system. Afraid of standing completely on my own two feet.

This was not the main reason why I felt trapped. To navigate the benefits system is complicated, over complicated. It makes little sense when you are trawling your way through the forms and guidance. You are treated as a number, for that is all you are. You learn very early on when accepting State handouts to never change your personal circumstances. For if you do the system can crash and deliver you an unbelievable amount of stress. Delays to your benefits, delays paying your rent. This leads to warning letters from your landlord and the council tax department threatening legal action. You try to find the sense in the system, but you fail, just like everyone else who has looked. You speak to benefit agency staff, they have no idea or control. Everyone seems to be waiting for the computer to make a decision. Once you experience the helplessness of being within such a system, you avoid unnecessary changes again. This means you do not rock the boat, you do not push yourself to take a chance or an opportunity. You become institutionalised. You live within the system and dance to its tune.

The best personal example I can give was the unsolvable issue of my council tax bill in the year 2000. I had spent most of the year technically unemployed and claiming unemployment benefits. I had signed off and then back on again probably a couple of times to keep the employment advisors off my back and to stop them sending me on a silly 'how to get a job' course. At the beginning of 2001, I got myself a job at Manchester airport for an airline. It was a proper job so I had to sign off the dole permanently. In April, I received a letter from the council stating that I was in arrears with my council tax bill. I knew this was correct and I was expecting such a letter. It was the amount they stated I owed which was the problem.

I cannot remember the exact figures anymore, so will use approximations to make my point. My bill for a full year was £1200. £100 a month. I lived alone so qualified for a 25% reduction. My bill was £75 per month.

I had worked for the last 3 months of that year so definitely owed £225. I would have signed off for a week here or there, but let us call it a month and add £75 to the bill. I owed about £300, probably under this figure. My bill official bill stated £575.

I wrote to the council tax office and gave dates of when I was claiming unemployment and therefore council tax relief. I gave all the information I had with a full explanation and figures. I received a letter back stating that I owed £575. No explanation. I wrote again asking for a breakdown of their calculations. Again they wrote back stating I owed £575.

I worked shifts and weekends, so knowing I was free on an office workday the following week I decided to visit the town hall and explain face-2-face. Letters were not getting me anywhere. It would be easier speaking to a real person.

I arrived at the town hall customer service section on the ground floor. The queue was long as expected. After 50 mins I reached the counter and a real person. I started my story. Once I said the words council tax, the lady interrupted me, gave me a ticket and told me to join queue three. I looked where she pointed and saw several more queues in different directions. This first queue was only to find out which queue to join for your particular inquiry.

Queueing in the second line lasted 90 mins. I finally got to sit down and speak to a real human being about my council tax bill. I explained my issue and why the bill was incorrect. I stressed I wanted to pay my bill, but just what I owed. The lady listened to my story and then typed on her keyboard. She looked up and told me I owe £575. I told her I knew how much the computer says I owe for I have a handful of letters informing me. My problem was the computer is wrong and I gave her my explanation. She looked puzzled. She told me she could not help and the best thing to do was to write to the council tax office and explain. I explained that I did that several times and never got a resolution. She shrugged her shoulders and said that she could not do anything further.

I was fuming. I had spent half a day at the town hall and got nowhere. I did not think my problem was complicated. It was just a matter of mathematics. Adding up the weeks I was officially unemployed and deducting the figure from the total. On the bus, on the way home I decided to pay the £575 bill. I did not owe this much, but taking into consideration how much I had taken out of the system it seemed a fair deal. It would put an end to the situation. Plus, I did not have the energy or time to continue fighting and complaining. The system wears you down. A decade later, when I worked for the council, I realised the systems are partly designed to reduce the call upon them – make a system difficult to use and people with minor problems will give up and go away. It worked on me!

If I could not solve this simple issue then how do you think people with poor communication skills and a lack of confidence cope in such situations? They do not cope. They become totally stressed and usually lose out on much-needed money or services. It is a lesson they do not quickly forget. The lesson learnt is never to change anything in your life again if it affects your benefits. This is also compounded by many similar experiences that are told by family and friends.

It is better to keep your hand stretched out in need than risk bettering yourself and losing out. This is the welfare trap.

I lived in this trap while growing up. It prepared me for a life on benefits. It enabled me to reject my personal responsibility, hold my hand out and beg. I feel ashamed as I write. In fact, I may never publish this chapter.

The irony of my experience is that every time I got a job, I excelled. I never failed or fell flat on my face. I always had what it took to be a success. I did not lack confidence or have self-doubt. I always knew I was special and amazing – I still do. My problem was I had been partly institutionalised by the State and was afraid of breaking free. Fear of the unknown. But like all children clinging to their mother's apron strings, eventually, I built up enough courage to break free and start my journey to adulthood. I was 30 years old.

What changed my state of mind? That is the million-dollar question. If I had a concrete answer I would be a millionaire for every western government would pay me well for my secret. The truth is everyone is different, every life is different. We are a creation of the combination of our genes and our experiences. Nature and nurture. I think what changed in me was my age, I turned 30 years old. I had told myself I would be a millionaire by this age. I was not. My financial prospects had currently dived as I had folded my small business.

Through an overheard conversation at a house warming party, I ended up with a job at Manchester airport. It was perfect for me. I could earn some money and access cheap flights to continue my love of independent travel. Both assertions turned out to be correct. This job started within me a process of unpicking my addiction to handouts and a lack of personal responsibility. My next job cured me completely.

I started work at a council, it was like working at the airport, it was just a job. But when I moved departments to the *Crime & Disorder Team* I found a career and finally meaning in my life. I saw in the young people I worked with what I had been decades before and was still fighting not to be again. I heard all my old excuses repeated back to me by these young people. I saw their fear of failure. I saw their intergenerational malaise. I saw their lack of aspiration. I saw their rejection of personal responsibility. I saw my life and mistakes reflecting back to me in the faces of every single young person who sat across the table.

I was a beggar for over half of my life. It is fact. I held my hand out to the State at every opportunity I got. Every penny given to me came with its own price, for it took away part of my agency and self-respect. I sold my soul. I sold it cheap.

I look back on the old me and I see someone who was just a taker. I was not a bad person. I had the same moral compass as I do now. The only difference was who I put first. It use to be me. Now I come second, third or fourth depending on the situation. Surprisingly, the lower in the pecking order I appear, the happier I seem to be. Go figure.

I have been a professional beggar. Paid to beg - begged for a living. I begged well. I created my own narrative to maximise the emotional impact on my preselected targets to loosen the purse strings of corporates and well-off individuals. This was my job for I was the CEO of a charity. I was the face of the charity. Founder and boss.

In the decade the charity has existed we have never paid for offices. I have always managed to get them for free. I have secured free accountants, free solicitors, free stationery, free laptops, free phones, free room hire, free lunches, free vehicle branding, free logo design, free website, free admin support, free IT support, and free wifi. This list does not end here, it can go on and on. The only thing I have never managed to secure for free is insurance.

Let us not forget the free money I have secured. *Individual donations online. Monthly direct debit. One-off corporate donations. Sponsorship. Raffles. Charity Balls. Parachute jumps. Sponsored events.* All begging. All carefully wrapped in a beggar's narrative to facilitate the handing over of cold hard cash.

My begging was fully legitimate. It was not a con or scam. My begging did exactly what it said on the tin. Every penny was spent running the projects at the charity. Projects delivering real benefits to specific individuals in the community. But every penny was secured through begging, let us not pretend otherwise.

Working for a registered charity, I had to follow certain rules and practices. A governing body had oversight over our actions and finances. Annual reports had to be submitted and made public, the same with our accounts. It is OK to beg if you are honest and do what you say you are going to do with the money. This means any money or resources are handed over with the full knowledge of how they are going to be used. This becomes a begging transaction, as opposed to a begging scam.

Recently, I have also become an online beggar. After I fought back from cancel culture and recovered from the ordeal, I wanted to take legal action against the two people who caused me the most trouble. Legal action requires money. I had resigned from my paid position at my charity and become Chair, for the charity was close to collapse due to the failings of the former trustees. I am not complaining, I was never about the money. To cover my legal fees I set up a *GoFundMe* account. Many people had followed my case, they felt the injustice and celebrated when I was ultimately successful in defeating the woke lunatics. Many people contributed to this fundraiser.

At the time of writing this book, I have forced an apology from *Dr Marilyn Comrie OBE* who dared to lie about me on *talkRADIO*. She has now retracted all her lies and the world now can judge her based on her behaviour and morality. Action is still progressing against the individual who set up the petition to have me sacked. For more on this part of my life read my first book: *Lessons In Courage*.

I also have used *GoFundMe* to raise funds to start a new project called *Go Woke Go Broke UK*. An online project to highlight companies that dare venture into the culture war and promote wokery. Checkout www.gowokegobroke.uk – *GoFundMe* did not like this project so kicked me off the platform completely. I would advise everyone not to use this platform going forward, it cannot be trusted. Have a look at how they mistreated the Canadian trucker protest in 2022 – they tried to steal their money. Disgraceful.

Learnt Helplessness

Learnt helplessness is a state of mind that can occur after a person has experienced a stressful situation repeatedly. They come to believe that they are unable to control or change the situation, so they do not try. Even when opportunities for change become available, they still do not try.

Neuroscience has recently provided more information about learnt helplessness and shown that the original theory was wrong – the understanding was backwards. It seems the brain does not expect to have control over stimuli, to think you may have control is learnt behaviour. The default position is to assume that control is not present.

Learnt helplessness is the subject's belief that their ability to achieve goals is insurmountable. It is a theory that clinical depression and related mental illnesses may be a result of a real or perceived absence of control over the outcome of one's life.

Summed up in one simple phrase: *What's the point of trying!*

A famous experiment by Seligman & Overmier involved three groups of dogs. This experiment would not be allowed today. The dogs were placed in harnesses. Group 1 were simply put in a harness for a period of time and were later released. Groups 2 and 3 consisted of connected pairs. Dogs in Group 2 were given electric shocks at random times, which the dog could end by pressing a lever. Each dog in Group 3 was paired with a Group 2 dog; whenever a Group 2 dog got a shock, its paired dog in Group 3 got a shock of the same intensity and duration, but its lever did not stop the shock. To a dog in Group 3, it seemed that the shock ended at random because it was their paired dog in Group 2 that was causing it to stop. Thus, for Group 3 dogs, the shock was inescapable.

In Part 2 of the experiment, the same three groups of dogs were placed in a box containing two compartments divided by a barrier a few inches high. All of the dogs could escape shocks on one side of the box by jumping over the low partition to the other side. The dogs in Groups 1 and 2 quickly learned this task and escaped the shock. Most of the Group 3 dogs – which had previously learned that nothing they did had any effect on shocks – simply lay down passively and whined when they were shocked.

In Seligman's hypothesis, Group 3 do not try to escape because they expect that nothing they do will stop the shock. To change this expectation, experimenters physically picked up the dogs and moved their legs, replicating the actions the dogs would need to take in order to escape from the electrified grid. This had to be done at least twice before the dogs would start wilfully jumping over the barrier on their own. Interestingly, threats, rewards, and observed demonstrations had no effect on the helpless Group 3 dogs.

A different experiment performed on humans had interesting results. A set of people performed mental tasks whilst subject to a distracting noise. Those who could use a switch to turn off the noise rarely bothered to do so, yet they performed better than those who could not turn off the noise. Simply being aware of this option was enough to substantially counteract the noise effect.

Research has found that learnt helplessness can sometimes only be relevant to a specific situation and at other times across many. People with a pessimistic explanatory style are more susceptible to learnt helplessness and are categorised by the following. Permanent - *it will never change*. Personal - *it's my fault*. Pervasive

- I can't do anything correctly.

Learnt helplessness may be a factor in a wide range of social situations:

- **Domestic abuse**. The victim accepts the abuse as nothing can be done to stop it.

- **Educational failing.** Students who repeatedly fail in the classroom concluded that they are stupid and stop trying to succeed. This results in increased helplessness, continued failure, loss of self-esteem and other social consequences.

- **Child abuse**. Neglect of a child can be a manifestation of learnt helplessness. When parents believe they are incapable of stopping an infant's crying, they may simply give up trying to do anything for the child.

- **Shy / Anxious.** In social situations, individuals may become passive due to feelings of helplessness. This can generate a negative reaction from others, which then reinforces the helplessness.

- **Old Age.** Individuals may respond with helplessness to retirement or the development of age-related health problems. This may cause them to neglect their medical care, financial affairs, and other important needs.

Social problems resulting from learnt helplessness may seem unavoidable to those trapped, but there are ways to reduce or prevent them. People can be immunised against it by increasing their awareness of real examples of where they were able to effect the desired result. Cognitive therapy has been used to show people that their actions do make a difference, this then increases their self-esteem and confidence.

Mental Health

Poor mental health played a large part in my life growing up. My grandmother, whom we lived with, was mentally ill. As a child, you think your life is normal or average. You do not know any better. You have very little to compare it to. I mentioned my grandmother in my first book and the crazy things we did to keep her calm. Writing about it opened a window into my early life and made me think about the long term effects of such an environment.

My grandmother was ill. Her mental health issues were not the new modern versions of anxiety, depression or gender confusion. She was mental. Invisible germs were everywhere waiting to get her - she was a germophobe. She also had *Obsessive Compulsive Disorder* - OCD, and she was a recluse.

I remember on many occasions hearing her screaming. '*The windows! The windows!*' - my mum would run around the house closing all windows for the weekly refuse collection was imminent and the large lorry was on our street. The lorry was a hive of germs. The action of emptying domestic bins into the lorry would cause the germs to go airborne and could come through the open windows. Danger.

I knew from an early age that she could not be left on her own. She did not like to be left on her own. Her eldest two children, my mum and an auntie, had very poor formal education because they were kept off school constantly to be a companion. They did the shopping as children for she rarely left the house. My mother contracted rheumatic fever as a child but no doctor was called - we did not allow strangers into the house. This illness damaged her heart, this would not be known for many decades later. My grandmother got worse over time.

I was not allowed friends into my home - I remember once having a birthday party in our garden shed. I had to sneak many items into my bedroom, including school books unless they were brand new. Saturday afternoons would be hell and explode after the weekly shopping was complete. Food prices increase over time. You tend not to notice if you shop every week for the increments are small and expected. My grandmother could not understand and would insinuate fraud by my mother, or whoever else had done the shopping. My sister and I would sit in our bedroom crying and holding each other as the verbally violent confrontations would be had. The irony was that when she died we found £7K in cash in her bedroom. Split into tiny amounts and squirrelled away in books, in pockets, under her bed and stuffed into ornaments. She probably had no idea she had any of it.

Her mental health issues ended when she quietly passed away in front of the TV, after eating a bowl of strawberries and cream. But the effects of her illness continue to be felt today in my family.

One of the biggest upsets in my family was a white lie that was never addressed. A grandchild out of wedlock brought up by my grandparents as their own. In my house, you never dealt with problems head-on for it was too emotionally distressing for my grandmother. We were taught to lie or ignore. This was how we kept the peace. Short term peace. Lies never remain secret forever. When the truth came out 15 years later, it severely damaged this child's sense of self and led to decades of forced isolation from her family and feelings of betrayal.

The daily news was never watched on our TV for it may contain a story that would cause my grandmother to worry and cause issues for everyone else. The accident at Chernobyl and the atomic cloud blowing towards England led to many changes in our household.

My grandmother and grandad had 3 children. All girls. My grandad was away a lot as he was in the Royal Navy and Merchant Navy. They lived in the same house but did not share a bedroom. They did not speak to each other or socialise in the same room. My grandad shared his bedroom with me and lived in the kitchen with a small black and white TV.

As I have explained, my mum and her older sister missed a lot of schooling because they were emotional support for my grandmother. This auntie was the firstborn and had a pronounced stutter – I developed the same infliction myself as a child. It seems obvious to me now that such a speech impediment was a direct consequence of the emotional trauma in the household. It affected the firstborn. Maybe children who come later have the advantage of learning to cope by watching their older siblings.

No education and straight into work do not lead to well-paid jobs or careers. Education had no value in my household. We never understood the potential it could bring to a poor working-class family, we had other problems to worry about. As the Welfare State grew after WWII we benefited - another reason why there was no need for education.

My sister and I had a very happy childhood. It was filled with pleasant memories, we were very lucky. Like many negative aspects of life, we forget the bits we do not want to remember. Whether we remember them or not, they still had an impact at the time and contributed to who we became. But I must stress that my childhood was very happy.

I see dysfunctionality in the three generations my grandmother left behind. It is not the same illness as hers, for she was old fashioned 'mental.' It is different now for it is purely behavioural - you could call it cultural. It is just what my family does. But the roots are firmly fixed in the behaviours we participated in to placate an ill woman. For the sake of kindness but more likely for convenience, we damaged ourselves in the process. We continue to pass this learnt behaviour down to the next generation and we watch them struggle. The only good news is that it is slowly diminishing over the generations. We are healing but it is taking time. The legacy of a very sick woman may one day finally come to an end.

Damaged families can damage family members, we need to figure out how we stop this cycle.

Human behaviour flows from three
main sources: desire, emotion, and knowledge.

- Plato

Chapter 3

The Begging Trinity

Begging is facilitated through social interaction. We are social creatures designed to live in small tribes and programmed to look out for other tribe members. This is one of the reasons why the idea of 'socialism' will not die. We know it does not work. We know it leads to atrocities, starvation and tyranny. Yet many people still want it, promote it and work towards it. This innate instinct to share resources and take care of other tribe members is a human trait. It is more prevalent in females for they had the role of child care, looking after extended family members and organising social events. A typical socialist is a blue-haired woman asking why we all can't just get along!

It is obvious that begging involves two people. It is a game for two. A 'giver' and a 'taker.' But have we missed someone out of the game. Is there a third player? Someone who may not even know they are taking part. Someone who is rarely asked to play but takes part nonetheless. Someone who may not even know the game exists.

A good beggar's narrative needs a baddie, someone to blame so the conversation about personal responsibility is not explored. *A patsy. A distraction.* A hero needs to rescue a victim from something tangible, dangerous or evil. Good can only exist in opposition to evil. There is no joy without pain. We are definitely missing someone from the game. We are missing a player. How can you expect to understand a game if you do not even know the basics, such as the number of players?

The *Karpman Drama Triangle* is a social model of human

interaction proposed by Stephen B. Karpman in 1968. The triangle highlights the destructive relationships that can occur among people in conflict. It can be used in almost any emotionally heightened drama or relationship.

He defined three roles in the conflict; Persecutor, Rescuer and Victim.

We find these roles in myths, legends and modern superhero films. Hero, Villain, Victim. Disney has their versions: The Handsome Prince, The Wicked Step-Mother, and The Damsel in Distress. Even cowboy films have a version: The Good, The Bad and The Ugly.

The Victim: This role is not necessarily representing a 'victim' in the true sense of the word. But can be someone feeling or acting like one. We have plenty of these types of victims in modern society. They feel victimised, oppressed, helpless, hopeless, powerless, and ashamed. They are unable to make their own decisions, solve problems, enjoy life, or accept personal responsibility.   The Victim will actively seek out a Persecutor to blame and also a Rescuer to save them. This reinforces the Victim's sense of helplessness and dependency.

The Rescuer: This role is all about enabling the Victim to be a victim and remain dependent. The Rescuer feels guilty if they do not go to the rescue. This behaviour does not allow the Victim to fail, learn from their mistakes and grow as an individual. Focusing on others in need allows the Rescuer to ignore their own anxiety and requirements. This role disguises the desire not to deal with their own issues as the Victim's needs are presented as more pressing and a priority.

The Persecutor: This role is about having someone to blame and at fault. They are controlling, critical, oppressive, angry, authoritarian, rigid, uncaring and superior. They have power over others and use it unfairly. They are everything dark within us.

A drama triangle arises when a person takes on one of the roles and attempts to recruit other players into the game. A Rescuer is usually the last to be found to complete the triangle. These roles can take on a life of their own and different outcomes can occur. The Victim might turn on the Rescuer, for example, while the Rescuer then switches to the Persecutor. People are complicated.

A reason the drama persists is that each participant is looking for their unconscious psychological needs to be met. They do not see or acknowledge the broader dysfunction or harm in the situation as a whole. They are acting upon their own selfish needs, rather than acting in a genuinely responsible manner.

The motivation of the Rescuer is the least obvious. They can have a complex mix of motives from being seen as compassionate and caring. They also can have a hidden motive to not succeed so their role continues or to succeed in a way in which they benefit. They may get a self-esteem boost or an increase in social standing by advertising how wonderful they are. They may derive enjoyment by having someone to help who looks up to them as superior. Our egos can be difficult to control.

The relationship between the Victim and the Rescuer is co-dependency. The Rescuer keeps the Victim dependent and in need by encouraging their victimhood. The Victim gets their needs met by relinquishing their personal responsibility by having the Rescuer take care of them.

The most basic way of explaining the dynamics of the three roles is through the family structure of father, mother and child. The Child is the Victim and demands to be looked after and taken care of. The Mother is the Rescuer and takes care of all the needs of the child. The Father is the Persecutor and pushes the child slowly towards independence. We are naturally predisposed toward these roles as adults. It is a matter of realising it, noticing when we are playing one of the roles, and potentially exiting the game if toxic.

Man owes his strength in the struggle for existence to the fact that he is a social animal. - **Albert Einstein**

The Begging Triangle

It was because I ran a homeless project on the streets of Manchester that I first came across the theory of the *Karpman Triangle*. I posted a tweet highlighting an issue I was having to educate the public on the complexities of the topic. Someone replied suggesting that I look into something called the *Karpman Triangle*. It blew my mind. I saw straight away how it fitted in with what I was witnessing daily. I realised that begging was not a game for two, but for three.

The 'beggar' is the Victim. Portrayed as an innocent player in the grand game of life. Persecuted by external factors with malevolent intentions. A pawn trying to stand up to a goliath but unable to progress. Open to accepting help from kind people who are stronger than them.

The 'giver' is the Rescuer. They take control of the situation. They give help and support, even if it is not wanted or needed. They are the protector of the weak and vulnerable. They push back against the malevolent forces that are laid against the victim.

The 'system' is the Persecutor. The 'system' can be the council, government or any other organisation. It can be the unfairness of life that allowed physical abuse, sexual abuse, or emotional abuse. It may be the incompetence of the justice system, social services or even our state education.

All three players are needed otherwise the performance does not work and falls apart. The most important and the least recognised is the Persecutor. Without this player, the other two roles are inevitably damaged and do not perform.

A beggar is not a 'real' Victim without a Persecutor. If no one is holding you back or keeping you down then the real persecutor in your situation is yourself. You must be lazy, stupid, inadequate, and to blame for your current situation. This is not a narrative that will generate support, sympathy and money.

A Rescuer cannot become a hero without a foe to fight and defeat. It is the act of placing oneself between a Victim and Persecutor for perceived unselfish reasons that enables the heroic crown to be earned. Without the illusion of self-sacrifice, a hero cannot be born. If hero status is not on offer, then there is no incentive to undertake the action for no positive emotional reward will be gained.

The Persecutor is vital. They are the kingpin of the game. They trigger our tribal protectionism. They fulfil our desire to seek out and overcome an enemy for we could be the next victim. We hear this all the time from 'givers' that it could be me or you on the street if circumstances unfolded differently - *'There but for the grace of God, go I.'*

The Rescuer: I give because I care

It feels good to give. That is why we give birthday and Christmas presents, especially to the people we love and care about. We want the birthday boy to be pleased with our gift, we want to see a huge smile - for this is our reward. Their positive emotional reaction triggers positive emotions within ourselves. We give to get. We are selfish creatures, we just do not realise we are. We all remember that person who did not give us a present even though we gave them one – it still annoys us today!

There is also social pressure to give. We have all purchased a Christmas present for someone we do not like because we felt we had to. This social pressure to be generous and philanthropic can be exploited. Have you ever sat in a pub having a drink with friends when a *'charity collector'* walks in shaking a donation tin? You see them out of the corner of your eye. You tense up. You hope they miss your table. They don't. You do not want to give. But the pressure to donate and put a few coins in the tin is overwhelming. If you can resist then good for you, for it is nearly always a scam and not a penny goes to charity. This type of giving is purely 'go away' money. We pay them to walk away and leave us alone. It is shame money. We hide what coins we are dropping into the tin, the amount does not matter, it is the act that is important - and the sound of the coins hitting other coins.

Why do people throw coins into paper cups held by dis-shelved homeless-looking individuals sitting on pavement corners? It is not the same as the pub example above for you can just keep walking past, avoid eye contact and away you go forever. No problem. There is something deeper going on with the individuals who give. They may be the best of us. They see humanity as it should be, as opposed to how it is. They want to help, but so do many other people who walk past or so they think. They are prepared and happy to help with a gesture, albeit, a useless one. One that actually makes things worse for the individual sitting on the pavement, but this does not matter for the donation was never meant to help the beggar. How can 69 pence in coins help anyone in the UK? Let us pretend you are drunk and you put £5 or even £10 into the paper cup. Do you really think this is going to solve any problem the person may have? Of course, you do not. It is similar to sitting in the pub, except this time you are not pushing back against external social pressure, but internalised social pressure. You feel guilty for the life you have compared to the person sitting on the cold wet pavement. You feel at fault for what you are spending on your lunch, your restaurant bill or your boozy night out. For a split second, you realise you are privileged and have no right to complain about the trivia in your life. Guilt diminishes and shame takes precedence. The quickest way out of this quagmire is to buy your way out. It is blood money, the amount is up to you. You are your own prosecutor and judge. It can be a brutal encounter. It may be difficult to lie to yourself, if you do manage it then a higher price to pay is down the road.

I have spoken to many people who happily give money or items to street beggars. They come in the following categories:

- **Pity**: they give because they do not know what else to do. They see someone in need and their reaction is to help. They have to do something, doing nothing is not an option. Giving a few coins is an immediate action and better than walking on by. These individuals usually want the best for the beggar and are open to new information from professionals if explained. Many will cease their counterproductive action if other more beneficial options are on offer and explained. They just want the person to be helped.

- **Selfish**: they give because the act of giving makes them feel good. It validates their own existence and achievements compared to the broken retch of a person in front of them. It gives them a sense of superiority. It gives them a real example of someone they are better than. These individuals do not really care about the well-being of the beggar. They are only looking out for themselves and how they feel. You can speak to these individuals until you are blue in the face, they do not want to listen. For if they listen to a professional they quickly realise they are not helping anyone and making things worse. This is not what they want to admit to themselves for it destroys their hero status.

- **Revolution**: they help because they know the people in power do not want them to help. It gives them a sense of rebellion and working against the system. *Sticking it to the man!* They are usually some sort of Marxist, communist or anarchist - scruffy with piercings is the best physical description. They do not care about the beggar. The beggar is just a tool to be levered to achieve their greater goal of a socialist utopia. They give the beggar no thought, they are irrelevant – a foot soldier in an invisible war. They are willing to actively harm the beggar if they think it will further their objective.

We all think we are in the first category, but as a professional in this field for two decades, I can say that rarely do I meet someone I would put into this category. The vast majority are firmly in the second category and a handful in the last. What we think we are is not necessarily what we really are, as defined by what we do.

Judge people on their actions, not their words. **- Anonymous**

Sometimes, our desire to be seen as a hero can cross a line. *Hero Syndrome* is a term used by media to describe the behaviour of a person seeking hero status or positive recognition. They actively create a dangerous or harmful situation for them to resolve. The term has been used to describe the behaviour of firefighters, nurses, police officers, security guards and politicians. Reasons for this kind of behaviour often vary. In an American study of more than 75 firefighter arsonists, the most common reason cited for starting the fire was simply the excitement of putting it out, not to cause harm or exact revenge.

Many people who actively put themselves in a rescuer position rarely do so quietly and without advertising the fact. They post photos of the good work they do and selfies with the Victims they are saving. There is a new phrase for this type of behaviour: *Virtue Signalling. Look at me and how amazing I am!*

Virtue signalling is a term used when one expresses a viewpoint with the intent of highlighting their good character to raise their social standing. It is a form of narcissism.

According to *The Guardian*, the term has been used since at least 2004. British journalist James Bartholomew is credited with coming up with it in an article where he describes virtue signalling as '*a public act with very little associated cost that is intended to inform others of one's socially acceptable alignment on an issue.*'

Virtue signalling has risen in popularity as social media has expanded. The term is used as a pejorative to describe such actions as posting a black square, a rainbow flag or stating your pronouns in your bio. Virtue signalling may incorporate some or all elements found in political correctness, self-righteousness, and moral superiority.

A more insulting similar phase is *White Saviour*. This term refers to a white person who provides help to non-white people in a perceived self-serving manner – it harks back to a time when non-white people were seen as inferior. The term is mainly associated with white middle-class people going to Africa to help 'the locals.' *Comic Relief* has been accused of this practice and has now stopped sending white celebrities to report on issues on the continent. It is argued that Africans find the saviour attitude of white people deeply patronising and offensive. Yet white people are continually invited and accommodated for they bring hard currency with them. There is a case to be made that this practice does not help and only teaches locals to be beggars with their hands stretched out to foreigners. Presently, China is trying to turn the whole African continent into beggars - are they *Yellow Saviours*?

I remember a conversation I had on a road trip in Natal in South Africa with a former British army officer who had retired and moved there.

I first met him in my hotel over a pint. He was a nice chap and offered to take me around the famous battle sites of the Anglo-Zulu war: *Rourke's Drift* and *Isandlwana*. It was during one of these trips that we drove near a Zulu village and stopped to let a group of children cross the road. It looked like they were coming home from school. They all smiled and waved. Some came over to look at the Land Rover, it was brand new and impressive. They did not speak English but were inquisitive. My companion started to hand out coins to the children. Some took them, some did not and some ran off – '*don't take money off strangers.*'

As we drove off, I tactfully raised the topic of begging and that the kids had not asked for money from us, but only wanted to meet us and look at the vehicle. He asked me to carry on. I explained that if we treat these kids as beggars by offering them money just for being black and poor, then this will create learnt behaviour for the future - linking free money to white visitors. He gave it some thought and eventually agreed it was not the right thing to do going forward.

Sometimes, there is no convincing someone that their misguided actions are contributing to the very issue they claim to be tackling. When this belief goes too far it can manifest itself as a *Messiah Complex*. Also known as a *Christ Complex* or *Saviour Complex* - a state of mind in which an individual holds a belief that they are destined to become a saviour. It can be identified as a category of religious delusion, they believe they are responsible for saving others. They have a strong tendency to seek out people who are in need of help, often sacrificing their own needs for these people. They may feel they carry the weight of the world on their shoulders, that their actions influence others and can change the course of society for the better. Individuals feel trapped as if there is no option but to take on the role of the 'saviour' to stop the suffering. If they do not act, who else will?

We're on a mission from God.
- Elwood Blues, The Blues Brothers

The best examples of such behaviour currently are connected to the environmentalist movement. Greta Thunberg has taken it upon herself to save the world – she is the Christ child. The modern *Joan of Arch* - instructed by God to fight his enemies and save mankind. A female *Noah* who has accepted the task of saving humanity from the oncoming destruction of rising sea levels, mass extinction and uninhabitable climate. This is not a new phenomenon, let us not forget the disastrous *Children's Crusades* of the 13th century to retake the Holy Land. Thousands of kids marched across Europe on their way to Jerusalem expecting the sea to part to facilitate their journey. They never left the continent. Many died. Others were sold into slavery when tricked onto ships for safe passage to the Levant.

It is easy to fall for such delusion when thousands of people are hanging on your every utterance. It is said that when the great Roman Emperor Marcus Aurelius walked the streets of Rome and engaged the adoring crowds, he would have a servant walk behind him and whisper in his ear: *"You are just a man!"* Our ego can be the destruction of us if we are not careful.

Now and again, the problem is a serious mental health disorder. A very close friend of mine told me about her experience with medical experts, concerning her son's ongoing poor health. To cut a long story short, they considered the possibility that she was responsible for the issues – she was not. They continued to investigate other avenues of cause. But this made me think about the possibility that 'kind-hearted individuals' may be purposely hurting rough sleepers or beggars so they have an opportunity to gain attention, a purpose in life, or even a sense of importance. This type of mental illness is called *Munchausen Syndrome By Proxy* (also known as *Factitious Disorder Imposed On Another*).

It is a condition in which a 'caregiver' creates the appearance of health problems in another person - typically a child by its mother. This may include actually injuring the child or just faking symptoms. The behaviour has no specific benefit to the caregiver, except for gaining attention and sympathy from medical professionals, family and friends.

What differentiates this from typical physical child abuse is the degree of premeditation involved. Most physical abuse towards a child is in reaction to a child's behaviour, such as crying or not doing as instructed.

Parents lose control and lash out, many regret the action afterwards. *Munchausen Syndrome By Proxy* is unprovoked, premeditated and carefully planned.

Health care professionals play an active role in the abuse, albeit unknowingly, by enabling the abuser. The caregiver will challenge professionals who will not seek further tests, drugs, procedures, surgeries, or referrals to specialists. They will also seek additional attention by making the medical system appear negligent for refusing to help a sick child. It is common for them to switch medical providers frequently until they find one that can be manipulated into a partnership of abuse. This practice is known as '*doctor shopping*' or '*hospital hopping.*'

The perpetrator continues the abuse because maintaining the child in the role of patient satisfies the abuser's needs. Even when the child is removed, the perpetrator may then abuse another child.

Some children learn that they are more likely to receive the positive maternal attention they crave when they are playing the 'sick role' in front of health care professionals. It is suspected that some Munchausen syndrome abusers may have been victims of the syndrome as a child. Seeking personal gratification through illness can thus become a lifelong and multi-generational disorder in some cases.

The Victim: None of it is my fault

Life is hard. Always has been, always will be. Technology may make it easier in historic terms, but we are not competing against people from a different time period. We judge ourselves based on what is around us now and what we see today.

When I read about Elon Musk and what he has achieved I feel like a failure. When I hear about a penniless immigrant who came to the UK and made himself a millionaire in one generation I feel I have let myself down. When I see on TV a council estate kid talking about attending Oxford University, getting a first-class degree and now being headhunted for an amazing job - I feel I squandered the chances I had. The only person you should compare yourself to is the 'you' that existed yesterday, last week or last year. Are you better than that version of you? That is the judgement you should make. Your personal development is the scale you use to judge your success.

The opportunities to feel bad about yourself never stop. But with a little work, you can twist any experience so that you are a victim of circumstance and not responsible for the outcome. Welcome to victimhood.

Victim mentality is an acquired personality trait where someone considers themselves to be a victim of the negative decisions of others and holds this view even when contrary evidence is provided. It is primarily developed from family members and situations during childhood.

They tend to believe that most aspects of life are negative and beyond their control, they deserve sympathy for their struggles, and they have little power to change things. This way of thinking is often linked to the experience of violence, crisis or trauma. It is a way of avoiding responsibility and criticism while receiving attention and compassion.

Personal characteristics of such individuals may include a lack of personal responsibility, seeing the worse in people, self-pity, seeking sympathy from others and believing other people are lucky. They are more likely to start sentences with: *I can't - I have no choice - I don't know.*

A telltale sign is the need to have their victimhood recognised and validated by others for this stops self-doubt and the need for self-reflection. If everyone says I am a victim, then I must be a victim. They spend their time focusing on the perceived unfairness rather than on solutions to their problems.

Begging For Racists

Let us start with some good news. It is now official – the UK is not institutionally racist. The *Commission on Race & Ethnic Disparities* (https://assets.publishing.service.gov.uk/government/uploads/system/upl oads/attachment_data/file/974507/20210331_-_CRED_Report_-_FINAL _-_Web_Accessible.pdf) released a report in 2021 that finally put this matter to bed in the minds of all sensible people. The UK is not a racist country – the debate is now over.

The race-hustlers are not happy with the report. They see their power and financial income threatened by the truth - for the truth will set people free. Only one option is available to them: attack and discredit the authors of the report. They tried, but the majority of people just smiled and saw through this performance. Race-hustlers will hustle; it is their nature.

A problem we have in the UK is a lack of racists, Nazis and fascists, for the demand for such individuals outstrips their true number. According to many race-hustlers, we have one on every street corner but I have never come across anyone who fits this description. They are an invisible enemy. Not one has ever tried to recruit me. They are invisible like institutional racism. Invisible like white supremacy. Invisible like the everyday racism that race-baiters see everywhere.

If black people are disliked in the UK today, why does black culture heavily influence our society? Music, fashion, language, films and sports stars. If white people are racist, why do they imitate something that they hate or do not value?

A century ago in America, we had examples of very light-skinned black individuals pretending to be white. This gained them advantages only available to white people. Many did so. But today, it is the opposite. Some white people pretend to be black to access benefits available only to non-white people. We have seen incidents of white academics stating that they are black to enhance their careers. Music artists do similar for financial gain. An American singer, Ariana Grande, has darkened her skin and changed her accent to move away from her 'white girl' image. British singer Rita Ora from The Voice has done similarly; both her parents are from Albania – not Alabama.

Even US presidential candidate Hilary Clinton changed her accent when addressing black voters. American Senator Elizabeth Warren had to apologise for claiming to be Native American. She had used this lie to benefit her advancement in several careers over decades. A DNA test stated that she had had a Native American ancestor probably 10 generations back. And let's not forget that many of our young people dress and 'act black,' for it is seen as cool and rebellious. This phenomenon is so common that a new word has developed to describe such behaviour. *Blackfishing*.

I do not remember reading about Nazis pretending to be Jewish for career advancement, or KKK members 'blacking up' so they could use the 'coloured-only' water fountains. There must be special benefits available to non-white people today in society. Otherwise, why are white people lying about who they fundamentally are? It now seems that being white may be a handicap.

Let me give you an example of one benefit of being black. Let us talk about the *N-word*. This is a word that cannot be used, spoken or referred to in full by anyone who is not black. It is a special word. A magical word. A black person can use it in a hit song, but a white person cannot sing it. This may be a silly example, but true.

Barclays, Deloitte and the BBC have all promised to recruit more black and brown people. They are not the only businesses stating this – many are. How do companies keep this promise? They do it by marking down white candidates during applications and interview selection. We use to have a word for this type of behaviour. If you want a better chance of getting a job at any of these companies, then it makes sense to pretend to be non-white. I have a family member who confided in me that they tick the *BAME* and *LBGT* boxes on all job applications. She is straight and white. Who would dare ask her to prove otherwise?

Many victims of racism I have spoken to discuss being called hurtful names. Name-calling is anti-social behaviour. *You fat bastard. You ginger bastard. You black bastard.* What is the difference? I am asking an honest question. They are all insulting, nasty, and hurtful. Why do we pick one phrase out and say this is the worst? Why is only one so serious that it needs reporting to the police? Why have we passed laws to tackle only one?

Have we not all called a loved one something nasty and hurtful? We may have regretted it later, but in the heat of an argument, our emotions can get the better of us. When angry, we search for the most hurtful thing we can say and then look for the reaction. We want to wound.

We want them to feel our pain.

When children engage in name-calling, we tell them to ignore it – *sticks and stones*. We have nursery rhythms about this type of antisocial behaviour. It has always gone on and always will. But we know how to stop it – we ignore it.

Black football players are currently highlighting the abuse they receive online. All football players receive abuse online. Social media brings out the worst in people. The game is a modern version of tribal warfare. Fans are taught to hate the other side, even if they are not playing each other that day. Football hooliganism is the apex of such tribal antisocial behaviour. Many footballers are targeted for how they look. Luke Chadwick, formerly of Manchester United, suffered years of abuse. It affected his confidence and eventually ended his career early. Constantly being referred to as ugly harmed his mental health – it destroyed him. The mainstream Press also engaged in this targeted bullying. If black players want the abuse to reduce online, then stop reacting to it. The more people openly discuss their hurt feelings, the more skin colour will be used as a weapon. The abuse is directed at black players from opposing teams, never at their players. Is this racism? Or just racist language? There is a difference. There is nothing anyone can do about this abuse online, except starving it of publicity. The *Beautiful Game* has not helped itself recently by supporting a racist, Marxist organisation – just saying.

Question:

A white man and a black man walk into a shop exactly at the same time for service. Who does the shopkeeper serve first? The white man because the shopkeeper thinks white people are superior? The black man because the shopkeeper does not trust black people to be unattended?

If you look long and hard enough, you can twist any encounter into a racist engagement. I feel this is what we have been doing for a long time in the UK. We use to call it *'playing the race card.'* The actor Sacha Baron Cohen highlighted this by creating a character with the catchphrase: *'Is it coz I is black?.'* I miss Ali G. I could relate to his take on urban youth culture. I never bonded with any of his other characters.

If you think everyone is racist, then when bad things happen, it is easy to jump to the conclusion that racism was the motive. You did not get promoted at work – racism. You see people whispering about you – racism. You do not get served in a pub quick enough – racism. You do not own your home – racism. Your life is a disappointment – racism.

Victim Mentality can be a comfort blanket, for it allows you never to take personal responsibility for your life. Nothing can be your fault, for the world is 'out to get you.' It is a solid gold excuse for your failures. The danger is that it becomes a self-fulfilling prophecy. Resentment grows and you become a bitter and unpleasant person. This ends up being the reason why people do not like you, not the colour of your skin.

We allow people free choice in the UK to pursue whatever they wish and to live their best life. But with this right comes personal responsibility. People will make different choices, for they are different. Similar people will make similar choices. This is the reason why we have different outcomes for different groups. British Chinese and British Indians outperform every other group in the UK. They value a strong, stable family structure and education. White British working-class do not and are at the bottom of education and earning power. This is not anti-white racism, just a lack of personal responsibility by a group that is similar in nature.

We need to stop looking for excuses for our failures and start searching for solutions so we do not fail next time.

Begging For Competence

Individuals can distort their reality. This is easily done if you have poor mental health, addiction issues, and historic trauma. It is called *Cognitive Distortion* - an exaggerated or irrational thought pattern that causes individuals to perceive reality inaccurately. A negative outlook on reality is a factor in symptoms of emotional dysfunction and poor mental health. Negative thoughts reinforce negative emotions. These thoughts can contribute to an overall negative outlook on the world and a depressive or anxious mental state.

An example of such distortion is *Stockholm Syndrome* - a condition in which hostages develop a psychological bond with their captors during their forced imprisonment. Emotional bonds are formed between captors and captives. These are generally considered irrational in light of the danger or risk endured by the victims.

In 1973, Jan-Erik Olsson tried to rob a bank but failed. He took four employees hostage. Three women and one man. The two criminals held the hostages captive for six days in the bank's vault. When the hostages were finally released, they would not testify against either captor. Instead, they started to raise money for their captor's defence fund.

Olsson explained his thinking in an interview with the police: "*It was the hostages' fault. They did everything I told them to. If they hadn't, I might not be here now. Why didn't any of them attack me? They made it hard to kill. They made us go on living together day after day, like goats, in that filth. There was nothing to do but get to know each other.*"

There are four key components that characterise Stockholm syndrome:

1. A hostage's development of positive feelings towards their captor

2. No previous relationship between hostage and captor

3. A refusal by a hostage to cooperate with authorities

4. A hostage's belief in the humanity of the captor

Stockholm syndrome is controversial. Not all mental health professionals think it is a genuine mental health condition. Instead, some think it is a coping mechanism when in potentially life-threatening situations. Similar symptoms are recorded in victims of sexual abuse, human trafficking, terror, and religious oppression.

Ronald Fairbairn published a psychoanalytic model in 1952 called *Psychoanalytic Studies of the Personality*. He explained the surprising reality that abused children become deeply attached to their abusive parents. This lack of positive emotional contact leads to the child being stuck at an earlier emotional age. They do not prioritise their own development for they are overly concerned with the whims, moods and emotional state of their abusive parent. They invest in keeping the parent happy as a survival strategy.

The abused child copes by 'not remembering' those events which are traumatic, as this awareness would be overwhelming. The child creates a false reality in which they believe that they are living in a loving and caring family. This is called dissociation, aka denial.

Evolutionarily speaking, Stockholm syndrome may be an inherited trait. Similar behaviour has been found in some reptiles and mammals. Abuse and subsequent submission and appeasement by the victim have been observed among chimpanzees.

Historian Azar Gat asserts that war and abductions were typical of human pre-history. Being captured by other tribes was a relatively common event for women. In some of those tribes, practically everyone was descended from a captive within the last three generations. Being captured may have been common. Women who resisted capture risked being killed and therefore not passing on their genes. A trait such as 'capture bonding' would contribute to the chance of surviving such an ordeal and the opportunity to produce offspring.

All animals have an innate drive to survive and to continue living. If we did not possess such a trait then our species would have died out a long time ago. We will do anything to survive. We will eat each other if starving, kill each other for resources, and even betray our loved ones if it saves our life.

How do you think people survived the Nazi concentration camps? They fought every day to keep death away. Why did they not just curl up in a ball, close their eyes, and wait for the end? Some did. Suicide rates were very high in the camps for obvious reasons – up to 25%. But that left 75% of prisoners unwilling to die at their own hands. They continued fighting to stay alive, in the hope that a better tomorrow would come.

Ahmed was referred to my charity by another homeless project.

He was living on a 'homeless bus' and needed a job so he could move on to more secure accommodation. The bus accommodated rough sleepers or those at immediate risk of rough sleeping. Beds had replaced seats on the double-decker.

We had many building firms supporting our homeless project. They would offer us low skilled vacancies such as labouring, cleaning, general duties etc. Full time and part-time positions. Part-time options were essential in some cases, an easier way to be introduced into the world of work.

We had a vacancy on our books for a cleaner to look after an on-site canteen. Simple cleaning duties to keep the tables and floor clean. The canteen was very busy as different teams of workers came in at set times. We interview Ahmed and offered him the job. He started the next day. Ahmed was unusual, for he was a British born Asian of Pakistani heritage. We had never before or since come across a British person of Ahmed's heritage rough sleeping.

Ahmed seemed fine and was a pleasure to chat to. He turned up, did his job and left. During one of our 'catch-up' sessions with him, to make sure everything was fine, he shared some of his troubles. He told us that where he was staying was run by racists, they treat him worse than a dog and they bullied him. They wanted to be rid of him. They did not feed him. The list of complaints was long, very long.

One of my managers paid a visit to the bus project to see what was going on. We had learnt not to take an individual's word for anything until proven. The partner organisation told us a different story. Their version was that Ahmed was not following the rules of the project. He wanted to stay in bed all day when not working. He wanted to cook his own food outside of kitchen hours. He constantly complained about the quality of the food on offer – even though it was free. And most importantly, he was not looking for his own permanent accommodation and was not engaging with his support worker. The project only offered emergency temporary accommodation until people found something more permanent. He had become their second-longest sitting tenant ever. Ahmed needed to find somewhere permanent and move on, so his place could be given to someone else living on the street and in need. He was bed blocking.

We spoke to Ahmed and discussed what we had found out. He was not happy that we did not agree with his assessment. We decided that his biggest problem was accommodation. He did not have a drink or drug problem, which was great, his problem was a poor attitude towards other people. We got housing benefits advice on what he would be entitled to and linked this in with what he was earning as a part-time cleaner. We enquired about a full-time cleaning position and were told that it could be arranged. This was looking easy. We knew there was no point in looking for shared accommodation for Ahmed. He had walked out of several previously for he did not get on with the other occupants. He needed a self-contained flat. More expensive but he would be working full-time.

We booked a meeting with Ahmed to discuss his options and see if he had particular areas he may wish to live in. Always involved people in decisions that affect them, otherwise, you risk removing their agency and chipping away at their confidence. The meeting did not go to plan. Ahmed had a bombshell that we could never have guessed existed. I still smile when I think about it and how this meeting progressed. I have never come across a more unique reason for not wanting to change your life for the better.

We discussed his financial situation. We explained we had a full-time job for him ready, what benefits he was entitled to, and that any flat deposit would be covered by the charity. His face was deadpan.

'What about my music studio?' he asked. I was puzzled. He read my expression. *'I told you about my music.'* He had. It was during an initial conversation when he told me he loved making music.

He then went on to explain that he had a music studio costing £400 per month. This was his priority. He finds the money every month. Nothing else in life mattered more than access to this studio. It is not very often I am lost for words, but Ahmed managed it that day.

That was the end of any productive discussion. He was adamant that he could not afford his own place once his studio costs were taken into account. He was not stupid, he was perfectly correct, the maths did not add up.

He was not with us much long afterwards. He got himself another part-time job deep cleaning commercial kitchens, it paid much better than our job. But it was not regular work, so when it conflicted with our job he started to phone in sick. We gave him an ultimatum, he left.

Ahmed's problem was a false sense of reality which affected his priorities. He saw the world in a way that makes no sense to us. Everything was about him and his dream of stardom. No one else's opinion mattered. He was quite happy to take a free bed and keep a rough sleeper on the streets if it meant he could still have access to a music studio. He would take free food for it saved him money. We had purchased additional food and left it in his locker at work so he could always have a lunch. It was just packets of cooked rice, baked beans and tins of tuna. Not a feast but enough not to go hungry.

How do you help a deluded individual see the bigger picture? How do you make them think about the long term, not the short term? How do you help someone like Ahmed? I still do not have an answer.

The Rescuer: I am Gandhi, Mandela, Dr King

We all dream of being a hero. We know it is a dream for we understand we would never put ourselves in harm's way for someone else. We may make an exception for a family member or best friend, but everyone else will have to fend for themselves. We know this to be true deep down inside. Only a tiny minority of individuals step forward when needed. Police officers run towards the sound of gunshots to protect, firemen run into burning buildings to find trapped people and carry them out to safety.

We watch action movies and want to be the main character. We suspend reality while watching and pretend we are them, we even think about what we would do in the same situation. We know it is not reality, we know heroes get hurt, we know we are just watching entertainment.

Nearly every myth and legend revolves around a hero. His birth, his upbringing, his acknowledgement of who he is. Tests and challenges are highlighted. Finally, the fight of his life emerges and he is successful. These heroes are nearly always male. This is also always the case as well in the modern world when we look for examples of someone putting themselves in harm's way. This does not mean females cannot be heroic or heroes, but life shows us it is nearly always men. Why? It is a way for men to gain social status – they risk their lives for the tribe. Women are too valuable to risk for they are needed to carry the next generation - men are expendable for they are replaceable.

The feminine version of a hero is one who self sacrifices through caring for others - the Mother Teresa effect. Queen Elizabeth I - did not marry so she could be the mother to the nation. Virgin Mary carried the son of God to save mankind from sin. Good mothers are a valuable commodity for they deliver healthy, productive children who will benefit the tribe. Women can raise their social status by highlighting how good a mother they are, we see this every day on social media. The competition between mothers is fierce. Stand at a school gate and listen to them passive-aggressively tear pieces out of each other based on mothering skills. *My child walked at 9 months. My child can already read. My child won star of the week.* This is all code for I am an amazing mum – some would say a hero.

A minority of people want to distract themselves from the battles they should be fighting if their lives are to be improved. Being a hero is a very tempting distraction. They are not stupid enough to walk around the streets at night like a vigilante looking for someone to protect from muggers and roaming gangs of thugs. They do not want to be Batman, so they settle for robbing the weak of their agency so they may feed upon it. Vampirism.

This may entail a mother who does everything for her son, she becomes a slave to his needs and through this develops a sense of purpose. She does not work, has no friends, no husband – all she has is her son and she must keep him happy or he may leave. Her fear of being alone clouds her judgement, she selfishly sacrifices her son's future happiness. I worked with a single mother and teenage son just like this scenario. She kept him under her thumb by constantly chipping away at his confidence. She would tell him how dangerous the world was. She heavily restricted his movements. He was incapable of making decisions, making friends, making eye contact, and making a life for himself. After several years of work, we raised his confidence and got him a job.

Every few weeks, I see on social media someone commenting that they do not mind when they give a beggar a few quid if they spend it on alcohol or drugs. Their reasoning is always that if they lived on the streets they would spend it on alcohol and drugs to numb the pain. Another popular opinion is once you have handed over the money then it is no longer your money, so you should not have a say on how it is spent. Both opinions have some validity, but neither actually helps anyone off the streets. They do confer a level of empathy and self-righteousness - for you must really understand the poor, the unfortunate and the downtrodden. You are standing up for the rights of a minority (the poor) and pushing back against whoever (the uncaring) is dictating what individuals should do. A quick post highlighting your morality with no thought to the damage it inflicts upon the weak is all you wanted. The comment receives lots of LIKES – validation of your amazingness.

Sometimes a Rescuer does not even want to be part of the game or triangle. They are co-opted through the use of pity, fear and even friendship. My friend Alex found himself in such a situation. His friend was using him as an alibi so he could cheat on his partner. Alex would get a phone call and then not be able to go to his local pub for the evening in case he bumped into his friend's partner. Alex was the Rescuer. His friend was the Victim because he needed a Rescuer to get away from his Persecutor. The partner was the Persecutor and had no idea what was going on. Alex eventually understood what he had gotten himself into and how he was enabling his friend to make poor choices. He put a stop to the *phone-an-alibi* service. His friend was not happy and so moved Alex from Rescuer to Persecutor, as he sought another Rescuer. To cut a long story short, his friend eventually told his partner he wanted to split up as he had not been happy for a long time. His partner agreed, and they split. Several years down the line, both have found new partners and are very happy. Alex's friend states that if Alex had not brought things to a head by refusing to be part of the lie, then he never would have had the opportunity to address his unhappy life. Collapsing the triangle forced his friend to accept his responsibility for his own happiness, instead of running from it.

Begging To Be Needed

We helped Jilly as a favour to the BBC. They were making a documentary series on the housing crisis in Manchester and wanted to follow Jilly from a squat to employment, to securing her own home by working with a charity. We were that charity.

Jilly was in her early 30s. We hardly ever worked with women for they have a special card to play in society when they are in trouble: children. This special card can stop you from being sent to prison, stops you from sleeping on the streets, and guarantees you a set monthly income. It is one hell of a card. Unfortunately for Jilly, she did not have custody of her child anymore.

She was the matriarchal head of her squat. She was the mummy bear. Her role was to look after everyone else, but never herself. She knew what she needed to do to get her child back, but something more important always came up. I have a family member in exactly the same position – sometimes the love of a child is not enough, hard to believe, but true. Ask any mother what they would not do to get their child back off the State? The answer is always the same. *'There is nothing I would not do.'*

Jilly was a nice person. Chatty, friendly, polite, confident. We arranged a job for her in the offices of the construction company where we were based as a *Trainee Administration Assistant* with other general duties. She lived opposite a tram stop so we purchased her a tram ticket to last a full month - future travel she would have to buy out of her wages. The BBC turned up many times over the following month to film her progress.

Women are different from men. I know this is almost illegal to say these days, but it is true. Jilly could not keep quiet. She could not stop speaking to people about her life, her experiences and her troubles. She disturbed people who were trying to work. We had lots of work to do to help her to develop a professional work persona. We failed.

She would not turn her phone off. She could not turn it off because people in the squat were dependent on her and she had to be available just in case of emergencies. They needed her and she loved that. The squat could not cope without her taking control and sorting out everyone and everything. Jilly wanted to be needed, she craved it for it filled a hole. She had replaced parenting her child with parenting a cohort of broken people. Female mammals who have lost their baby will often allow other babies to suckle, sometimes even different species. The maternal instinct is strong.

Her phone would ring and she would answer it immediately. Conversations would range from what name someone had just been called, to how much cannabis they had for that evening. She even had a conversation one day about if she could bring home (steal) some toilet rolls from work because they had run out and no one wanted to waste money buying them. Some conversations were more violent and contained threats, verbal outbursts and the use of profanities were frequent. This would happen while she was standing in the middle of the office or the staff kitchen. Phone calls were never urgent or an emergency, but rather they were gossip and the latest drama in the squat. It was a soap opera. A never-ending litany of meaningless drivel that offers a sense of importance. The company bent over backwards to support Jilly, the office manager was fully onboard and handled any internal complaints about her behaviour. A softly-softly approach was taken to improve her work ethic and professionalism. The company knew it was going to take time and was willing to invest in Jilly for a reward in the medium term.

Within two months she had resigned. She gave two reasons. She was struggling to pay for her daily tram ticket and the people in the squat needed her more than she had realised.

We had spoken to her and offered advice about how to save some money to buy a monthly tram ticket which worked out a lot cheaper than buying one daily. But instant gratification from a pay packet always took precedence. She could not turn down cannabis today for more cannabis next month.

The dependency of her squat-mates was an illusion or had been fostered at best. They did not need her, she needed them. She was the top cat in the squat. At work she was on the bottom of the ladder, she knew it, she was not stupid. She had a choice. To be a big fish in a small pond or a small fish in a large pond but with the potential to grow.

She needed to be needed. She needed a role in life where she felt valued. She preferred to be childless and beg for State handouts and pity, rather than to take the more difficult path of personal responsibility.

Trevor was a nice man. A genuine man. He was not homeless and had never pretended to be so. He just wanted to help others. He had suffered a huge personal loss in his life and this empty space needed filling. He found purpose and meaning by speaking to homeless people on the streets - he would try to help them by buying them socks. Unsurprisingly, it did not matter how many pairs of socks he bought, the hosiery did not help anyone off the streets and into a better life.

Trevor's life was falling apart. His mental health was poor. He neglected himself for other people took priority. He would not deal with his personal loss for it was too difficult. It was easier to surround himself with people more broken than him. This made him feel less damaged and more normal. It also kept him busy which meant he had an excuse not to delve into his own issues, find solutions and improve his own life.

He needed the rough sleepers more than they needed him. In fact, they did not need him at all. He offered them nothing they wanted, except a few pounds if their beggar's narrative was good. He was susceptible to female beggars. His 'male protection' instinct would kick in and his wallet would come out. Nothing sinister on his part, just a good man trying to help vulnerable women.

He created himself an avatar online and gave himself a cool title that advertised what he did on the streets. His whole life was this avatar. His whole life was on the streets. Deep down within his psyche, he did not want to eradicate rough sleeping, for this would eradicate his own existence. He was trapped in a symbiotic relationship. Or more truthfully, he was in a parasitic relationship, he fed off the misery of others. He was of course, unaware of this state of affairs, he truly believed he was helping.

Sometimes, it does not matter how hard you try, you cannot get that hero feeling. The first project I created to work with rough sleepers was completely run by volunteers. I advertised for interested people online, conducted interviews and arranged a training session to go through policies and procedures. We started with three people.

One of these new volunteers was a local university student, another eventually became the full time paid manager of the project. The student attended many shifts and increasingly became frustrated with the project and her involvement. After two months she resigned. The reason she gave was that she had not helped anyone since she started volunteering, and it looked like she never would for the project did not achieve anything.

She wanted to be a saviour, a hero, a doer of remarkable things that save lives. She wanted to be the Greta Thunberg of rough sleeping and lead people to the land of beds and roofs. She must have originally thought that rough sleepers were stupid and could not figure out how to ask for the help on offer. Or that the council and other services were purposely not helping rough sleepers for some unknown reason. She had wanted to be either the conduit into accommodation or the social justice warrior taking on the council. She wanted quick fixes and quick emotional rewards. It was perfectly clear to see that her offer of volunteering was really all about her. Her gratification. Her emotions. Her sense of importance. Her.

We do not have any social issues in the UK which can be fixed quickly, easily or just with money. If we did they would have been fixed by now. Life is complicated. Problems are complicated. People are complicated. One 20-year-old uni student will not change the world, but she could have stayed volunteering and potentially contributed to positive change in one person's life – that would have been something to have been proud of forever.

Persecutor: I didn't know I existed

This is the hardest role to explore for in many cases it is a ghost, an apparition, or completely made-up. It is wrong to say that this role does not exist, for if a person believes a Persecutor exists then they change their behaviour accordingly and the same outcome is achieved. It does not matter if you do not believe in Father Christmas if you still get presents under the tree.

We can all exhibit traits of a Persecutor – I am susceptible to the third trait below.

Control Freak: needs to be in control of everything and have things done their way. They take charge when not happy with the method and blame others. New ideas are rejected unless they bring them to the table.

Moody: makes others walk on eggshells to ensure they are not upset or triggered. They can create a negative atmosphere through passive-aggressive body language, toxic humour or cynical comments.

Silent Treatment: withdraws and cuts off interaction as a way to punish others and control the situation. This can create a negative atmosphere where others are powerless to address it.

Manipulation: uses their personality or status to gain influence and access to power to further their own negative agenda. Befriends those who are helpful to their agenda, and ignores those who do not. This creates an atmosphere of mistrust.

In the context of this chapter, we mean a Persecutor who treats people cruelly and unfairly. Over my two decades working with individuals who see themselves as victimised, the usual suspects of Persecutors are the council, the government, the police, social services, the justice system, their parents, their family, their former partner, an abuser or just old fashioned bad luck.

Let us explore a couple:

The Council: if you are looking for someone to blame for your misfortune or state of affairs then all forms of government are perfect. Who has not had a terrible encounter with the government? Who has not watched a government crisis unfold on TV and thought they could do a better job? We all have. I spent a decade working for a council, here are a few of my favourite personal examples of a system that does not work and is incompetent.

I need a £1 picture frame from a pound-shop for a certificate I made to give a kid who did something wonderful. I asked for petty cash and was refused by the office manager. But she said she would order me one online right there and then. She was true to her word and printed me off a receipt for my budget records. The cost was £15.99. Where is the sense in this purchasing system?

As a new idea, I wanted some large plastic banners to place across the side of police vans when they were parked up at community events. A good way to advertise a crime prevention message. We were only allowed to use the internal council printing team for such requests. They informed me that they had a new line in banners: magnetic. They could be rolled out and stuck to the side of a van in a matter of seconds. They were expensive but sounded perfect. I ordered two. £1200. When they arrived we tested them, but they did not work. I complained and was told they were not for vans with uneven surfaces. They were dumped in the bin.

When a rough sleeper explains that the council cannot help them off the streets, most people believe the reason. For they know the council does not function well, and probably have their own silly stories of council incompetence.

The council may be incompetent but they are not intentionally malicious or staffed by Nazis. Many good staff try their hardest to help people in need within a system that is not fit for purpose. I know many of these people, they struggle daily to do their best, and many leave disillusioned or burnt out. The people who stay tend to be the ones who care less for it is easier to cope if you are less empathic. Even these staff are not Nazis and still care.

Family: this is another good Persecutor to blame for it pulls at your heartstrings. Families are supposed to love you, be there for you and look after you. How can a parent or a family be so evil, reject you, beat you, abuse you? We read about such families almost weekly. A single mum allows her boyfriend to beat her child to death and then lies to protect him. Sometimes the mum is the abuser, other times it is an uncle engaged in sexual abuse for a decade. A more common issue is parents handing over their child to grandparents to raise, so they can continue living their life the way they want.

All of the above are genuine reasons why someone may be damaged, in pain, and in need of help and support. I have come across them all many times. But this does not always give you the full picture of the family situation, even if we accept that what they say is based on the truth.

Let me tell you some of the reasons parents and family members have told me when I asked for their side of the story.

He constantly stole from me for drugs, he even stole my mum's wedding ring and sold it. That still hurts today.

I helped my brother out when I could. I use to cook for him if he was hungry and occasionally let him sleep on my sofa. The final straw was when I was burgled and my neighbour told me she saw him climbing out of the window.

He pawned everything of value I owned that I was not currently using.

She was a nightmare. Always drunk which usually led to violence and the police arriving.

When he came to visit we would remove all pocket-size valuables and bottles of alcohol and lock them in my bedroom.

He punched my husband, his stepfather, many times – finally I had enough and threw him out.

There are three sides to every story – yours, mine, and the truth.
- Robert Evans

*Shame is like everything else; live with
it for long enough and it becomes part of the furniture.*

- Salman Rushdie

Chapter 4

A Lack Of Shame

We have no shame – shame is dead in the UK. We eradicated this 'so called' social virus over many decades. Shame does not sit comfortably within the new environment of equity, diversity and inclusion. It was perceived to be holding people back in life, was unfairly discriminatory and seen as old fashioned and even backwards. In many ways, the people who promoted this understanding of shame were correct. But every action creates a reaction. The unintended consequences of social change are never contemplated, planned for or mitigated. Thousands of years for our culture to develop to where it is today and we think we can make changes with no negative impact or reaction. We are naïve and foolish.

Definition: shame is an unpleasant self-conscious emotion typically associated with a negative evaluation of the self; with feelings of distress, exposure, mistrust, powerlessness, and worthlessness. 'To shame' generally means to actively assign or communicate a state of shame to another person. In contrast, to have no shame is to behave without the restraint to offend others, similar to other emotions like pride or hubris.

When I was a child in the 1970s, I was told to never bring the police to the door of my home. The neighbours would see and gossip about the morality of my family. They may comment on the effectiveness of the parenting on offer, and decisions would be made if other children were allowed to play with me. I did not bring the police to my door – except for once but they were the Park Police who were council security guards. I was caught messing around on a boating lake and climbing onto the special bird preserve island.

My friend, a few doors away had the police at his door many times. His older brother was a low-level criminal. My friend and his younger brother were both on their way down the same path. Their father had died suddenly and their mother could not cope with 3 boys who were already a handful. It all went downhill fast. I remember going into their home one day and seeing hundreds of boxes of cigarettes piled up on the coffee table. Loot from the burglary of a local corner shop the night before. Another time, I helped myself to several bars of chocolate from two boxes stolen from a corner shop storeroom. My friend had 'lifted' them while preparing newspapers for his paper round. The funniest sight was when the older brother ran down my street to his home with a sheep carcass on his shoulder. A local butcher had taken too long to sort out a delivery to the shop and the refrigerated van backdoor was left unlocked. There was no shame felt by this family, as far I could see. It was normal. It was acceptable. It was learnt behaviour. You could say it was their culture.

Decades later, I worked with many family-support professionals who seemingly were trained to blame all negative behaviour on an unfair society. Sexism and racism were the most common. But not understanding cultural differences was a great excuse if the family were not white British. It was the same in the 70s – maybe not as prevalent. The victimhood culture had already begun. My friend's family could not help it for they were poor, lived in a council house, and now was a single-parent household. This bigotry of low expectations did not help anyone. My street had several families in the same situation and they were not dysfunctional – my family included. We may have been beggars but we were not antisocial.

Up to my friend's dad dying, I was the only kid I knew who did not have a father. My parents separated when I was two and I never saw him again. I was the exception, not the rule. Now we have removed all shame around being a single parent, we have seen an explosion in single-parent households. To help women who made poor choices, we created thousands more of them so they would not be lonely. Currently, approximately 15% of all families are lone parent households. What we know for sure is that this type of family unit delivers the worst outcomes. Worst for the taxpayer, for society and most importantly, for the children who are deprived of a biological father living with them. Yet hardly anyone says anything about it.

By the time I reached my late teens and was able to sign on the dole, society's opinion about claiming unemployment benefits had changed. In the early 80s, the unemployment rate was very high as Margaret Thatcher remoulded the economy. Millions were unemployed through no fault of their own. It was not a case of laziness – there was a lack of jobs, especially in certain geographical areas. It took many years for new jobs to be created. New jobs were not evenly distributed across the country, some areas were left decimated and are still suffering today.

This period of our recent history removed our sense of shame around claiming benefits. We are now told that we are 'entitled' to the money and it is there for us to claim. It is our right. The money belongs to anyone who fits the criteria. Once we accepted we are entitled, the next question is: '*Am I not worth more than this?*.' Beggars now place a monetary worth upon themselves. They assign a value to their life of inaction with no sense of gratitude or responsibility. And definitely with no sense of shame. It has become normal. It has become a lifestyle choice and many people have opted into this life, or more accurately, been trained for it.

Begging For A Tribe

Shame is a social construct. Its job is to control the behaviour of individuals for the benefit of the wider good, to ensure peace and foster prosperity. For most of our existence, we lived in tribes and faced danger from every possible side. Everything was out to kill us. The only way to survive was for the tribe to work together. To all pull in the same direction and avoid internal conflict as much as possible. Actively shaming miscreants was the tool we used to achieve a semi-harmonious state. Later, some of this developed into religion, superstition and laws.

It makes sense to reduce the number of incidents that have the potential to cause internal strife within a tribe. *Stealing. Infidelity. Lying. Laziness. Assault.* A tribe cannot fight an enemy if they are already fighting between themselves. It is amazing that our societies were ever created at all - given the human propensity for violence, greed and antisocial behaviour. Societies that cannot control these instincts soon degenerate. This is what happened in Northern Ireland, Cyprus, Yugoslavia, and Rwanda.

Nobody wants to work hard all day while gazing upon others doing less for the same benefit or reward. This breeds resentment and bitterness – which leads to violence. But on the other hand, no one wants to see another tribe member starving to death even if it is their fault. This problem is highlighted in *Aesop's* fable of the *Ant and the Grasshopper.*

One bright day in late autumn a family of Ants were bustling about in the warm sunshine, drying out the grain they had stored up during the summer, when a starving Grasshopper, his fiddle under his arm, came up and humbly begged for a bite to eat.

"What!" cried the Ants in surprise, "haven't you stored anything away for the winter? What in the world were you doing all last summer?"

"I didn't have time to store up any food," whined the Grasshopper; "I was so busy making music that before I knew it the summer was gone."

The Ants shrugged their shoulders in disgust. "Making music, were you?" they cried. "Very well; now dance!" And they turned their backs on the Grasshopper and went on with their work.

This is the problem that socialism can never address – personal responsibility. Socialism is an upscaled version of tribal life. All societies require tools to control individual behaviour for the perceived greater good. We saw what these tools were in socialist societies in the 20th century – they were deadly. Not everything can be upscaled successfully. Not everything that works at the micro-level can perform at the macro-level. Once a certain capacity is reached within traditional tribes they tend to split into two. The bigger the tribe the further you are away from the centre. The less chance you know the people making the decisions. The less chance the people making the decisions know you personally and take your individual needs into account. You become a metaphorical number.

I remember working with many white middle-class teenage girls in Manchester city centre over many years. Young people from all over Greater Manchester would gather in a specific location on a Saturday afternoon to socialise and have some fun. The area was called *Urbis* – also known as *Cathedral Gardens*. A city centre is not a place for kids to hang out, especially middle-class kids with no street sense but plenty of valuables. Many were robbed every week – that is a story for another day. The girls I spoke to would talk about how they did not fit in at home or school. They referred to themselves as *Emos*. They felt different. They felt special. They did not want to follow the crowd, they wanted to be unique. They achieved this by dressing like every other teen in this location. They all looked and sounded the same. They all listened to the same music, used the same slang, acted the same and looked the same. Their original tribe was too large, they felt insignificant and ignored. But this new tribe was much smaller so they felt part of it. We all want to belong. We may not realise we do, but we do. The harshest punishment we hand out to incarcerated criminals is solitary confinement, we would not do this if it was not effective. Remember that we are social creatures.

Every tribe needs rules. Young people flourish when they have clear and enforced rules. Societies are no different. Without rules, you cannot play a meaningful game for no one knows what anyone else is doing. Life without rules degenerates into violence - survival of the fittest is the default setting. Uncooperative societies die out fast for there is no trust or goodwill, only conflict. Women and children do not last long in such environments.

For you to survive the tribe has to survive. For the tribe to survive, you have to contribute to the tribe.

My Personal Shame

As a child I was not ashamed of being poor, I did not realise I was. Some friends got bigger and better Christmas presents than me, but they did not go on holiday every year like me. Some years I had 3 holidays – a week at Butlins, a week in Ireland to see family, and a week abroad on a school trip.

Having a stutter growing up was hard. Dreading every situation that I knew would come along where I had to speak to an adult I did not know, for this would trigger my speech impediment. It was embarrassing, occasionally funny, and always left me feeling ashamed and a bit of a freak. I was ashamed of my grandmother due to her mental illness. All my friends knew she was mental, it only really became a problem in my mid-teens when I started to bring girls home. It did not stop me from bringing dates home, I would explain the situation and then try unsuccessfully to get them naked. Hormones do not care about your problems.

I regularly feel shame when I have underperformed and let myself down. My A-level results are a good example, I achieved one grade C and two grade Es. This was the first time I truly realised that I had let myself down and potentially damaged my future by not working hard enough. I knew I had made too many excuses, and pursued too much pleasure – I had been a grasshopper. I failed because I had personally failed. I felt the same when I had been unsuccessful at promotion interviews at work. My fault. My failing. A sense of shame that I could not convince the interview panel that I was the best person for the job. I knew I was the best person, but let myself down by not proving it.

I remember in my early twenties, I had my own flat and worked on the markets as an independent trader. Times were tough. Some days I would be lucky to earn enough money to pay the stall rent and restock. I started to enter any free competition I saw in newspapers or magazines, but only if it was free postage for stamps cost money. This was before the National Lottery, it was my way to try to generate some good luck. One morning I opened my post. I had won a competition. It was not the top prize of a million pounds or the second prize of £100K, but a runner up prize of 25p. The cheque was enclosed. This sounds funny until you realise that the following week I cashed it so I could buy a loaf of bread for 19p. I was penniless that week. I remember standing in the *Abbey National Build Society* paying in the cheque, waiting a few days and withdrawing 25p. Both visits to the branch were painful, embarrassing and shameful that I needed 25p. I look back at this incident and become angry with myself for being ashamed. The cheque was mine. It was legal tender. I needed the money. A shop got an extra sale and I got the opportunity to make some sandwiches. What was there to be ashamed about?

Once I started to become successful with the charity, I found myself in many situations where I felt I did not fit. *Black tie gala dinners. Charity balls. Speaking to politicians, CEOs and millionaires.* I felt my accent would single me out – I sound common. To overcome this I always try to dress up and present myself as professional. For the record, my accent has never singled me out. It is just paranoia on my part. A chink in my armour - my *Achilles' heel.*

Shame is a soul eating emotion. - Carl Gustav Jung

The most recent bout of shame I suffered was my public cancellation in June 2020. It nearly broke me. Falling from my pedestal hurt. Watching everything I had built crumble into dust before my eyes. Listening to hundreds of people on social media calling for my sacking, misunderstanding my words, insisting that I was not only wrong but a racist and a Nazi. This is hard to take the first time it happens for we are programmed to take on board criticism from others. This is how we regulate our behaviour within a tribe or community so we do not incur its wrath. A fully functioning individual will take on board what others say about them, you would be a fool not to. It hurts when someone tells us something negative about ourselves. It can upset us so much that we break down and even cry, it does not really help if we know it is not true. To have one of our peers judge us is terrifying. Now imagine it is hundreds of people, all saying you are not a good person. It does not matter that it is only on social media, we react the same way as if they are at our front door with pitchforks and flaming torches.

I was convinced people were laughing at me, mocking me, celebrating my downfall. Some probably were. I wanted to curl up in a ball and disappear. It felt like my world had ended. I blamed no one but myself. I was ashamed of myself for being such a fool and allowing the events to happen. Taking responsibility can hurt, but it is the only way forward.

Begging For Fair Play

Women's sports is the latest nirvana for a category of athletes we use to call 'cheaters.' Today, we call them trans-women athletes. As I write this, we have a complete mess in US college female swimming where men are smashing all the female records. And the unbelievable sight on YouTube of men beating the crap out of biological women in combat sports.

In 2021, a New Zealand trans-woman (biological man) weightlifter was selected for the Olympic Games in Japan – a Tongan woman stayed home with her ovaries. A moment in Olympic history? Is this similar to Jesse Owens in 1936 Munich? Or the black power salute of Tommie Smith and John Carlos in 1968? Or maybe even the convicted murderer Oscar Pistorius, who competed in the 2012 Games with artificial legs?

The Olympics may be the ultimate stage in world competition, but they have had their fair share of cheats. We are complicated animals and for some, cheating seems an acceptable path. We are all treading the line between what we crave and what we know is moral. The most common form of cheating is performance-enhancing drugs. Sometimes administered by the State as in the recent case of Russia, but usually by the athlete and their coaches. But not all Olympic cheats take drugs – some are old-school, they cheat by rigging equipment.

In the 1976 Olympics, Boris Onishchenko entered as a three-time world fencing champion for the Soviet Union. During a match, the rival team protested that Onishchenko had registered a 'hit' without his sword actually touching his opponent. It was clear to see that Onishchenko's sword was in the air when the 'hit' registered. Upon investigation, it was discovered the sword had been illegally modified. A switch had been added that, when pressed, registered a 'hit.' Onischenko was ejected from the Games in disgrace.

The Paralympics are not exempt from cheating. In the 2000 Games, Spain was stripped of their intellectual disability basketball Gold medals. An undercover journalist revealed that most of the team had not undergone medical tests to ensure that they had a disability. It transpired that the required mental tests, which should show competitors have an IQ of no more than 75, were not conducted by the Spanish. It was also alleged that some Spanish participants in the table tennis, track & field, and swimming events were also not disabled either, meaning that up to five more medals had been won fraudulently. It was confirmed later that 10 out of the 12 members of the basketball team were not disabled.

A good thing about the Paralympics is that it shows that everyone is vulnerable to making poor choices, regardless of physical ability. 'Boosting' is a term used to describe a type of self-harm performed by athletes with a spinal cord injury. This can increase their blood pressure and enhance performance. It is done before or during an event. Techniques include over-tightening leg straps, electric shocks and even breaking toe bones.

The most famous cheat in my lifetime was Lance Armstrong. An American former professional road racing cyclist who won the Tour de France seven consecutive times from 1999 to 2005. Armstrong was a sports icon. He had already beaten testicular cancer a few years before he conquered the world of cycling. He was seen as a national hero and an example of what can be achieved with hard work and perseverance.

A doping investigation concluded that he had used performance-enhancing drugs throughout his career. He was also named as the ringleader of "*the most sophisticated, professionalised and successful doping programme that sport has ever seen.*" Eventually, he acknowledged his involvement. His reputation was destroyed. He was stripped of all his titles and given a lifetime ban from cycling and any other sport.

If you want to see professional athletes cheating today then just watch a game of football, especially Latin teams. They tumble over as if shot by a sniper, roll around in agony, then jump up and run the length of the pitch. It is all a performance to con the referee into awarding a foul.

The best example of this is Rivaldo, a world-class Brazilian player, in the 2002 World Cup. The game had briefly paused, a Turkish player angrily kicked the ball at Rivaldo who was waiting to take a corner. The ball hit Rivaldo on the knee. He hit the ground instantaneously while holding his face. The Turkish player received a red card and was sent off the pitch. The con worked – Brazil won the game. The public outcry was huge, for it was captured on TV and the whole world saw it. Rivaldo was fined £4,300. He never apologised.

As an Englishman, I cannot talk about sporting cheats without mentioning Maradona and the *'Hand Of God'* incident. In the 1986 World Cup, Maradona jumped into the air to head the ball. His arm rose above his head. The ball hit his arm and rolled into the back of the net. Goal!!!!!

No – of course not. It was an infringement of the rules. The game is called 'football' for a reason. Maradona did not acknowledge this infraction, he just celebrated his non-goal. In this particular incident, he had not intended to cheat, it was not premeditated. But cheating it was. He later stated that the incident was the 'Hand of God' intervening in the game. He never apologised.

Winning isn't everything, it's the only thing.
- Henry Russell Sanders

Why do people cheat? Is it for fortune and glory? At the highest echelons, the difference between first and second place is often millions of pounds and a significant amount of fame.

Psychologists can split athletes into two groups. Task-oriented athletes focused on hard work and self-development. Ego-oriented athletes focused on being better than everyone else. According to the *Handbook of Sports Psychology*, studies have shown that highly ego-oriented athletes have lower sportsmanship, more self-reported cheating and an endorsement of cheating.

Any notion that cheaters feel guilty after engaging in unethical behaviour is simply not true – it is the opposite. Cheaters usually report no negative emotion over their actions, but can report positive emotion if successful. This is called a 'cheater's high.'

Is cheating worth it when the risk of getting caught is always present? In a BBC interview, Lance Armstrong said that if it was still 1995, he would *"probably do it again."*

What does all this boil down to? A lack of shame. When we eliminate shame from society we enter the world of Mad Max where anything goes. Without societal rules, I do not know what you are going to do, so I must expect the worse if I am to survive. I have to protect myself, my family and my possessions. Act now, ask questions later. A dangerous way to live your life.

Begging Chinese Style

We hear a lot recently about communist China's social credit system and how they reward good behaviour but also punish poor behaviour. A modern way to control the population: a new carrot and stick.

The problem China is trying to address is what does a country do when its citizens have a lack of trust in each other? Plus, no trust in the government. How do you conduct business when you think the other person is going to rip you off? How do you guarantee good quality products or services? How do you get people to act the right way for the greater societal good?

Most societies use shame and social pressure to make individuals conform – such rules are called norms and traditions. The Chinese are attempting to use modern technology to achieve the same result, for something went wrong in their culture. Remember that all cultures can be broken by the people.

Why does China have a trust deficit? It may have something to do with the lasting effects of the decade long *Cultural Revolution.* Friends and family members were pitted against each other, loved ones report each other to the police, and everyone was a potential government informer. In this type of environment, trust is difficult to foster. Societal shame becomes unimportant for you have much more serious considerations to ponder that may inadvertently lead to you being reported to the police for sedition. A slip of the tongue could end your life.

Different social credit systems are running in China today:

Business trustworthiness system: blacklist system for discredited business organisations. Violations include not paying taxes, producing low-quality goods, and disobeying environmental protection policies.

Government trustworthiness system: evaluation system targeting civil servants and government institutions. This category attracts the second-highest number of enforcement actions.

Social trustworthiness system: blacklist system for discredited individuals. This includes antisocial behaviour, playing loud music or eating on public transport. Violating traffic rules and jaywalking. Making reservations at restaurants or hotels but not showing up. And failing to sort personal waste correctly.

Judiciary public trust system: blacklist system for discredited individuals. 'Deadbeat debtors' are advertised. Citizens are encouraged to report individuals who they believe could repay their debts or fines.

Punishment for poor social credit includes increased audits and government inspections of businesses. Reduced employment prospects and exclusion from high-prestige work. Travel bans, slow internet connection, exclusion from hotels, and public shaming.

Rewards for positive social credit include less frequent inspections and audits for businesses. Fast-tracked approvals for government services. Discounts on energy bills, being able to rent bikes and hotels without payment of a deposit. Better interest rates at banks and tax breaks.

As of 2019, 27 million air tickets and 6 million high-speed rail tickets had been denied to people who were on a blacklist. Personal information of blacklisted people is publicly accessible and advertised. This may be online but also at various public venues such as movie theatres and buses. Some children of blacklisted individuals are banned from attending private schools and universities.

Can anyone argue against this system in China? Do we not have similar systems in the West? The punishing of children for the sins of their parents is a bit harsh and goes against our sense of justice. But are not children of prisons punished for their parent's lawbreaking? Separating children from their parents causes huge emotional damage.

The real issue people have with this social credit system is that it is linked to the apparatus of mass surveillance run by an authoritarian State. Every country keeps tabs on its citizens for many reasons. The question is when does it go too far?

All citizens in China are required to carry a national ID card – many countries do. The new generation of cards will be able to track movement. These cards are the only acceptable form of identification. They are needed to purchase plane tickets, high-speed train tickets, financial services, education and healthcare. Real name registration is mandatory for internet access. Purchasing a SIM card requires a facial recognition scan so the mobile phone number is linked to a real identity.

In 2018, law enforcement officers were equipped with facial recognition 'smart-glasses' to apprehend criminals. Two years later, they were given 'smart-helmets' equipped with AI-powered infra-red cameras to detect pedestrians' temperature amid the coronavirus pandemic. They also had facial recognition capabilities, license plate recognition and the ability to scan QR codes.

Skynet is not just the computer system from the *Terminator* films. It is also a Chinese system of facial recognition cameras used to combat crime. Citizens are identified through cross-referencing with national databases held by the government. *Sharp Eyes* project monitors all public spaces using surveillance. It aims to *'closely guard against, and crackdown on, the infiltration, sabotage, subversion and separatist activities by hostile forces.'*

Police Cloud is a system to collate data from healthcare, social media and internet activity. It has access to residential addresses and family relations. Personal information like birth control information, religious affiliations and biometrics. Plus hotel & flight records, train records and CCTV footage.

Digital Yuan is a pilot digital currency issued by the *People's Bank of China*. Widespread adoption would theoretically allow authorities to see economic activity in real-time and offer many benefits in managing the economy. But it would also give the State the power to turn off access to money for people deemed problematic or criminal - comply or starve. This is an immense power to wield.

The State needs to be able to manage and control its citizens – this is common sense. How to do this while balancing civil liberties, public protection and the rule of law is complicated. It is becoming more so as technology allows new options to be implemented that were only seen in sci-fi films a few years earlier.

People want to be safe and will always look to the State or a tribal leader to provide such safety. We are happy for the liberty of others to be curtailed and even removed if we think it will make us safer. A problem only occurs when it is our rights that are removed. When it is personal and detrimental to our life – then it is an issue and has gone too far.

We do not need to look towards China as an example of where State power has become too big and powerful. We are less free today in the UK than we were a decade ago. *Hate speech. Covid restrictions.* The government of Canada has frozen protesters' bank accounts – comply or starve. Let all this sink in and then say it is only the evil Chinese communist government.

Begging To Be Seen As Normal

For shame to be ineffective as a tool to control people's behaviour and actions, it must be widely shown that such behaviour is common, normal and mainstream. You cannot feel shame for something that everyone does and talks about.

The Jeremy Kyle Show was a popular talk show presented by Jeremy Kyle and produced by ITV Studios. It premiered in July 2005 and ran for seventeen series until its cancellation due to the suicide of a guest. It was the most popular daytime programme for ITV. The show was constructed around promoting confrontation between guests, usually family members or partners. A friend worked opposite the TV studio where the show was filmed. She said you knew when they were filming this particular show for the street was full of mentally ill-looking individuals queuing for a place in the audience.

The show was a modern-day version of bear-baiting. It took low intelligent, dysfunctional individuals with deep-set emotional issues and encouraged them to display their dirty washing publicly for the whole world to see - and laugh at. *Alcoholics. Drug users. Abusers. Mentality impaired.* A fuse would be lit and then the invited lunatics would perform for the TV audience. *Arguments. Accusations. Insults.* And if lucky - fights. *Who stole grandmother's drug money? Did Pete sleep with his mother in law? Will grandad marry his 17 yr old step-granddaughter?* It was pure entertainment derived from the misery of others. The audience would laugh, boo and jeer as if at a pantomime - in some ways it was a pantomime.

Shame is a terrible thing. Necessary, but terrible.
- James Frey

'*Schadenfreude*' is a German word, loosely translated as *Harm / Joy*. It is the experience of delighting in others' misfortune. Experiencing pleasure from the troubles, failures, or humiliation of others. It is a complex emotion. Rather than feeling sympathy towards another person, pleasure is taken from their misfortune. This emotion is displayed more in children, as adults tend to hide it.

One of my favourite quotes reflects this meaning well.

It is not enough that I succeed, but all others must fail.
- Genghis Khan

Research has found that there are three driving forces to such mentality:

1. **Aggression**: primarily involves group identity. The joy of observing the suffering of others comes from the observer's feeling that the other's failure represents an improvement or validation of their own group's status.

2. **Rivalry**: is individualistic and relates to interpersonal competition. It arises from a desire to stand out from and out-perform one's peers. This is based on another person's misfortune eliciting pleasure because the observer now feels better about their personal identity and self-worth.

3. **Justice**: comes from seeing that behaviour that is deemed as immoral or 'bad' is punished. It is the pleasure associated with seeing a person 'get what they deserve.' People feel that fairness has been restored for a previously unpunished wrong – we call it karma.

Research has shown that individuals with lower self-esteem tend to experience the feeling more frequently and intensely. Those with higher self-esteem experience it less frequently and less intensely.

Schadenfreude is the perfect word for shows like Jeremy Kyle. The show gave the audience a line of freaks, fools and idiots to point out and laugh at. The audience feels better about themselves for no matter what 'bat-shit crazy' stuff is taking place in their life, they know they must be normal for they are nothing like the freaks on the stage. Fraudulently claiming benefits is normal compared to sleeping with your grandad. Paying for a bit of heroin at weekends using your child benefit payment is normal compared to prostituting yourself 12 hours a day to pay for the same habit.

The ultimate crime of this show, and many others like it, is that it has normalised dysfunctional lifestyles and behaviours to such an extent that they are no longer shocking to us for we have seen worse. When something is seen as normal the controlling ability of societal shame is removed.

These types of shows can also be referred to as *Freak Shows*. In Victorian times there would be an exhibition of biological rarities, referred to in popular culture as '*freaks of nature*.' Typical features would be those uncommonly large or small, conjoined twins, those with intersex variations, and those with extraordinary diseases and conditions. Not all abnormalities were real, some were fake (just like on Jeremy Kyle according to many accusations). Heavily tattooed or pierced people were displayed. As well as specialist acts like fire-eaters and sword-swallowers. People felt that paying to see the show permitted them to compare themselves favourably to the freaks.

A showman (presenter!) would oversee the unveiling of the 'freaks.' The show would include costumes, choreography and performances. Exhibits were authenticated by doctors who used medical terms that added an air of authenticity.

Freak shows were a valuable form of amusement for the middle-class and were profitable. Some argue that freak shows were also beneficial for people with disabilities, giving them jobs and a steady income. Others argue that the showmen exploited vulnerable individuals for profit. Both arguments are probably correct.

The entertainment appeal of the 'freak shows' is seen today in TV shows such as *Extraordinary People* and *BodyShock*. Participants are portrayed as individuals, not as exhibitions. But the motivation of people tuning in to the TV show is plainly obvious.

Not everyone who looks upon, or is interested in, people struggling in life are doing so for purely negative reasons. Sometimes it is for the novelty factor or simply curiosity.

Poverty Tourism is a type of tourism that involves visiting impoverished areas to see 'how the other half lives.' Originally, starting in the slums of London and Manhattan in the 19th century, slum tourism is now prominent across the world.

During the 1980s in South Africa, black residents organised township tours to educate the whites in local government on how the black population lived. Such tours attracted international tourists, who wanted to learn more about apartheid. I attended such a tour when I visited the country in the late 1990s. It is still big business. In Cape Town, over 300,000 tourists visit the city each year to view the slums.

Poverty tourism is used in many forms of entertainment, aka ghetto tourism. Gangsta rap, video games, movies and TV all use poor urban locations for entertainment value. A way to experience the life, dangers and deprivation of the inner city from the comfort of your own home – risk free. After *Hurricane Katrina*, tours were offered in flood-ravaged sections of New Orleans. The hit TV show *The Wire* led to tours of the drug-induced ghettos of Baltimore. The film *Slumdog Millionaire* increased the demand for tours of the slum areas in Mumbai.

A 2010 study by the *University of Pennsylvania* showed that tourists in the slums of Mumbai were motivated primarily by curiosity, as opposed to other factors such as entertainment or education. The majority of tourists reported positive feelings during the tour, with interest and intrigue as the most commonly stated feelings. It seems many tourists visit the slums to put their own lives in perspective. The study also found that most residents of the slum were ambivalent about the tours – like fish in an aquarium.

Slum tourism has been the subject of much criticism, hence the term *poverty porn*. The primary accusation against slum tourism is that it turns poverty into entertainment and is used to feel better about one's own life. It is ultimately a selfish interest. The counterargument is the tours provide employment and income for the slums by selling souvenirs, refreshments and other items.

As a society, we may be getting more technologically advanced, but do not confuse this with becoming more intelligent. The latest research into human intelligence is that we are declining, probably due to who is reproducing. Higher IQ people have fewer children compared to lower IQ individuals. We are not breeding superhumans, we are breeding out intelligence genes. Mother nature use to take care of our gene pool by adding a little chlorine to eliminate the defective and stupid. Today we ensure everyone survives childhood and has the opportunity to pass on their genes – I am not advocating against this. Simply put, 200 years ago in the UK the child mortality rate was at 31%, 100 years ago it was down to 14%, today it is 0.4%.

We keep messing with things we do not know the consequences of. This does not mean we stop 'messing with things' for this is called progress, but we need to be aware of unintended consequences and mitigate against them.

> **Don't remove a fence until you understand why it was put there.**
> **- G K Chesterton, 1929**

We keep ripping up fences and are then surprised when we realise the fence was actually needed and had a purpose. We currently see this with the gender ideology mess we are in. That was why we created sex-based roles in society, so everyone knew their place.

The Swedes have a very interesting word, *'fredsskadade,'* meaning *'injured by peace.'* It is where society has been prosperous & peaceful for such a long period of time that it somehow hurts them through ignorance and complacency. The lack of strife handicaps them. They are not prepared for change or an attack. *Fredsskadade* is made up of the words *'fred'* which means 'peace,' and *'skadade'* which means 'damaged.'

This word is perfect for describing what happened to the Dodo – it had its own way for so long that they were unable to adapt to new predators or competition. Dodos would walk up to hunters to see what was going on. They had no instinct to be afraid. There is a valuable lesson contained in the phrase *'Dead as a Dodo.'*

I first heard the word *fredsskadade* by accident on Twitter. I was writing this book and the word jumped out at me as very relevant as I read a post. You have to be careful when online not to believe everything you read without confirming it elsewhere. I once forwarded a tweet announcing the premature death of Margaret Thatcher by Sky News. It was a joke account. I made myself look very foolish for many people shared it, including the police. *Fool me once, shame on you. Fool me twice, shame on me.*

I googled the word to check but all results came back in Swedish. It may come as a surprise to many, but I do not speak Swedish. I barely speak English. I used google translate but the word itself must have been translated with the rest of the text for I could never find it in a document or webpage. I put a shout out online for a Swedish person to help me. A friend of a friend answered my call, she confirmed the validity of the word.

The heart of manipulation is
to empathise without being touched.

- Vernor Vinge

Chapter 5

A Political Beggar

Politicians are the kings of the 'beggar-makers.' It is in their interest to create voters who owe their fealty to an individual politician or political party. They achieve this by creating and fostering dependency, in fact, it is better described as co-dependency. One begs for votes, the other begs for favours. The power dynamic flips between the two depending on the timings of the political cycle. It is big business.

Professional lobby groups 'unofficially' buy the support of politicians on particular issues with promises of campaign donations, which are spent on re-election. A politician may speak out on an issue just to generate support from an identified group of potential voters. Stopping the deportation of foreign criminals seems crazy and a vote loser. But if you think you will benefit from an increase in support from a particular ethnic group of voters, then it makes perfect sense.

Governments themselves play this game. They float the idea of a potential new policy to see if the public like it. If they do, then great – if not, it is scrapped immediately and a statement is released saying the policy was never going to be implemented anyway. This is how cowardly our politicians have become.

This is how politicians get votes in the UK: they beg, trick, con, buy and steal.

When it comes to fostering fealty within the general public and specific identity groups, they have become masters. The best example of this is the welfare system – a tax-funded benefits system that traps people in poverty and allows the middle class to feel good about themselves.

All the main political parties have their eye on this issue and how it affects potential voters. The *Labour Party* actively tries to buy votes with increases in benefits or new benefits to be applied for. The *Conservative Party* used to have a different approach – they would sell the idea of aspiration and working hard to be successful. But now they seem just like every other socialist party and plough more money into the system for a quiet life, while our national debt mounts.

The Road To Wigan Pier

George Orwell's book of the same title is a good insight into the poverty of northern industrial towns in the 1930s. My town. My life if I had been born 30 years earlier. Put into this context it was a scary read for me. It changed my view on the welfare state.

The poverty highlighted in the book was striking. Life was hard for most people, some more so than others. Working in the coal mines was tough work, backbreaking work, all in the knowledge that tunnels caved in and exploded frequently. Having to crawl for almost a mile to reach the coal face before you officially start your paid shift, knowing you have to crawl back at the end of your shift.

Families living in small damp houses infested with bugs. Two or three people to a bed. No central heating. No inside toilet. No bathroom. This was normal life up north and most of the country. These people were looked down upon by the metropolitan elite in London - some things never change, Brexit showed us that. It was a common joke at the time to say that there was no point in giving Northerners bathtubs to improve their hygiene, for they would only store coal in them. The level of disdain was palpable.

Orwell also discussed how these working-class people liked the idea of socialism but did not like socialists. For they felt the same disdain from socialist activists as they did from the bourgeoisie. Again, some things never change.

This book is a good remedy for anyone who thinks we do not need a welfare state or government intervention in social issues. Any thoughts I had of such an idea were eradicated while reading the book.

The argument is not should we have a welfare state or not. But rather, should our welfare state deliver a handout or a hand-up. My answer has always been a hand-up, for handouts have the capacity to foster dependency and ultimately create beggars. As you know, I speak from personal experience.

We owe a debt of gratitude to the *Political Left* for fighting for a better tomorrow for the working class. They fought for our future even though they never knew if we would exist. They fought for democracy and took the head of a king in the process. They protested unfair laws and changed them. They demanded equal rights and got them. Slowly but surely, they were successful. Every step forward improved the lives of everyone who came after. It was a journey, not an event.

I live around the corner from *Peter's Field* in Manchester. This is the site of the infamous 1819 *Peterloo Massacre* where approximately 18 people died, including an unborn baby. Armed cavalry soldiers charged into a crowd of 60,000 people who had gathered to demand parliamentary reform so working-class MPs could vote against the *Corn Laws*. These laws benefited rich landowners by keeping the price of cereals artificially high. It was not in the landowners' interest to allow cheaper wheat to be imported to enable cheaper bread to be produced.

A few minutes away from *Peter's Field* is the *Mechanic Institute*. This is where the *Trade Union Congress* held its first meeting in 1868. The TUC took the leading role in fighting for better working conditions, fair pay and employment rights. Today, the TUC brings together unions to draw up common policies, lobby government and campaign.

Manchester was at the heart of the fight for a better tomorrow and a higher standard of living for the working class. This fight was taking place everywhere. Let us look just up the road at the *Rochdale Pioneers*. They founded the modern cooperative movement in 1844 to provide an affordable alternative to poor quality food. Any surplus profits were used to benefit the local community and people.

It was a proper fight to gain ground to improve the lives of the working class. An example of the pushback from the powerful is the *Tolpuddle Martyrs*. Six agricultural labourers from a village in Dorset. In 1834, they were convicted of swearing a secret oath as members of the *Friendly Society of Agricultural Labourers - a* forerunner to trade unions. They were arrested on a legal technicality during a labour dispute against cutting wages and were convicted. They were sentenced to penal transportation to Australia. Deported from their own country! This is what tyranny looks like.

Life is not fair. We are not all treated equally for we are not equal. We are not all born with the same privileges or opportunities in life. The state should aim to level the playing field as much as possible, but a completely level will never be achieved. It should not pull others down to level the field, but rather raise people by offering opportunities. It should offer hand-ups, not handouts. Compensation for being dealt a poor hand in the game of life is not needed or beneficial. But the offer of help so you can improve your skills and circumstance is a sensible gift to give.

So allow me to be clear for my detractors - we need a welfare state. I do not wish to live in a society where people can fall upon hard times through no fault of their own, hit rock bottom and never have the support to recover. I have seen real poverty through my travels. I have read about historic poverty in the UK. I do not want any of it.

Handout or hand-up? That is the question we need to ponder.

A paper cup welfare system

Everyone in the UK wants a welfare system. They may disagree on how it should work, how much money to spend on it and who to target, but overall the need for a system is universally accepted.

The question we need to ask is why do we want a welfare system? Is it to simply help the poor to avoid abject poverty? No one wants to see starving people on the streets, that is enough to put you off your dinner. Maybe it is to give people a hand-up to better themselves? Or is it to remove the responsibility from the unintelligent in running their own lives because the State can do it better? I do not think it is any of the above. The reason we all want a welfare system is that it makes us feel better knowing a system we fund through taxation is there to catch vulnerable people. We pay guilt money so we can enjoy the pleasures life offers us. This is why we seemingly do not care that the system does not work for the people it is tasked to help.

Our welfare system is like a paper cup in the hands of a beggar. We put a few coins in it and absolve ourselves of any duty of care or responsibility for others. We feel better through our taxation but have no real desire to help the individual. We pay for our peace of mind and a comfortable night's sleep.

If we wanted a welfare system that solved problems then why does our system fail to solve problems? If it is to reduce poverty then why do more people every year enter the welfare system and receive support. Why is poverty intergenerational? Why are we constantly finding new poverty issues to solve without solving the ones we have had for decades?

The care of the elderly is a massive problem in the UK. It grows annually as the population ages. Like all social problems we have brought this upon ourselves by ensuring older people are healthier than previous generations, so live longer. Surely this is a good thing? But at the same time, we have dismantled the traditional family structure and left our ageing parents to cope for themselves as we pursue our selfish dreams and needs. We place them in care homes and pay the bills so our conscience is clear. We pray the care home does not appear on the news highlighting the physical and emotional abuse of residents. Or we leave them to live alone in the old family home and convince ourselves that it is for the best, as it is familiar and full of memories. Many rely on the State to pick up the bill for their care, some complain that it does not do enough. The well-being of our loved ones is now the responsibility of the state. Old people have become a hindrance. They have become unwanted and treated as refuse for the State to sort out.

Tackling social problems is difficult and complex. Politicians know this and therefore try to resist the temptation of trying to fix them. It is easier to throw money at the problem as a sticking plaster and walk away. I spent a decade working with politicians and what they always wanted was a problem to be perceived as solved. It did not matter if it was or not, it just had to look like it was. Politicians are nourished through public opinion, it is manna from heaven, without it they are not politicians for much longer. Keep the voters happy. Notice that I said voters and not people, there is a huge difference in a democracy. It has always been as such, hence why sharing the right to vote was fought against.

Unintended Consequences

Many governments have encouraged people to ignore and violate the moral principle that it is wrong to live at other people's expense.

Every government has introduced new social policies or tinkered with existing ones. Their intentions are always good, but remember the road to hell is paved with good intentions. What is the outcome every time we remove an evil dictator from a Middle East country? Exactly. When we change very complicated systems that we do not understand, we have no idea of the outcome in the medium and long term. In many examples, we have no idea in the very short term, such as Iraq and Libya.

In such systems, where it is impossible to account for every reaction to a change then we enter into the field of *Chaos Theory* - a branch of mathematics that looks at complex systems whose behaviour is extremely sensitive to minor changes in conditions. Small alterations can give rise to much bigger consequences. Remember the assassination of a Duke no one had heard of, in a place no one can find on a map? It led to WWI and the death of 40 million people.

The most well-known part of this theory is called *The Butterfly Effect* - the idea that small actions can have non-linear impacts on a complex system. The concept is imagined with a butterfly flapping its wings and causing a typhoon. Of course, a butterfly flapping its wings cannot cause a typhoon. But small events can influence other events that eventually can set the stage for something large to take place, such as a typhoon.

The easiest way to understand *The Butterfly Effect* is the following proverb which can be traced back to the 14th century in English and the 13th century in German.

For want of a nail, the shoe was lost.
For want of a shoe, the horse was lost.
For want of a horse, the rider was lost.
For want of a rider, the message was lost.
For want of a message, the battle was lost.
For want of a battle, the kingdom was lost.
And all for the want of a horseshoe nail.

Small things matter – we know this to be true. We sometimes struggle to explain it, but we intrinsically understand it to be true. My personal favourite of related sayings that try to educate us on this truism is '*Look after your pennies, and the pounds will look after themselves*' – I know this to be true and live my life by it.

When I was responsible for Manchester city centre in terms of reducing antisocial behaviour, I received many complaints from a well-known supermarket chain. This led to local councillors on my back. The supermarket was fed up with beggars outside a particular shop annoying customers. This was a fairly common issue and I knew what to do. I included the location on the local police patrols and asked the council rough sleeping team to visit to engage and offer support. After a month of action, it was still a problem. The supermarket was not happy. At this time, begging was not a huge issue in Manchester (hard to believe today), we had plenty of resources and staff – I was perplexed.

I am a hands-on type of person. You have to see and feel a problem sometimes before you can solve it. I visited the supermarket and stood across the road to see what was going on. I then sat with the beggars for a chat and asked if they need any accommodation help or any other support. None were sleeping rough.

After 45 minutes in total at the location, I entered the shop and asked for the manager. I had solved the problem. The manager appeared, I introduced myself, and he remembered me from our email exchanges. We sat in his office and I explained why he had a problem and why it was all his fault. It was his turn to look perplexed.

The beggars were very comfortable sitting outside his shop. This was now not a surprise to me for his security team allowed them to use shopping baskets as seats while sat begging. They turned them upside down and a seat was created – better than the hard cold floor. He was shocked. I continued.

Any sandwiches, pastries, and pies that were removed from sale due to the 'sell by date' were automatically offered to the beggars outside. The same shop that was constantly complaining about the individuals sitting outside annoying customers was actually feeding the individuals they were complaining about. Some staff were even purchasing specific items that were requested and handing them over, such as soft drinks and even cigarette roll-up papers. I finished ruining his day by passing on the only complaint the beggars had about the shop – '*They will not let us use their staff toilet.*'

Eventually, the manager smiled and thanked me. He knew what he had to do to solve his problem. He did it, for I never saw another report logged from the shop about begging.

Small acts of 'so called' kindness led to complaints from customers about antisocial behaviour. Why? Because the chain of events that would take place by being 'so called' kind was never considered, understood or expected - *The Butterfly Effect.*

A few years ago, I was watching a documentary on TV about the war in Afghanistan and how difficult it was to fight the Taliban on their terms in a guerrilla war. A British army officer gave a personal story of how little they understood the Afghan people, their culture, and what they really wanted in life. As a sign of goodwill, his soldiers built a water well in a small village in the middle of nowhere – part of the winning of hearts and minds strategy. What possibly could be wrong with such an act?

Every few weeks the soldiers would visit the village as part of their patrols. The village elders would report that the well was not working which meant that the women still had to walk to fetch water every day. Rumours were whispered that the Taliban were sneaking into the village to damage the well, but this made no sense for the damage was always minimal. Surely the Taliban would blow it up and make the villagers watch?

On one particular visit, the well needed fixing again so the army officer set his men to the task. He took this opportunity to walk around the village with his Afghan interpreter to smile at people. He found himself chatting with a small group of women. One of these women suddenly burst into life vocally, his interpreter translated as fast as he could. The woman was very clear in her demand.

She told the officer to stop fixing the well. None of the women wanted it, they never asked for it, and they did not want to use it. The officer was shocked. Was she a Taliban sympathiser?

She explained her position. The daily chore of fetching water was the only time of the day that the women were allowed to leave the home and socialise. The time spent at the river was an opportunity to talk, laugh and feel alive. When the water well is working this part of their daily life is removed. This is why the women of the village have damaged the water well and will continue to do so. The women then disappeared before they got into trouble.

The happy ending to this particular story is that the soldiers did not manage to fix the water well that day. It looked like they had at one point, but further tests directed by the officer proved otherwise. A new part from the UK was needed and would be ordered. For the remaining of the officer's tour, the spare part never arrived at his base, so the water well was never fixed. After a few months of excuses, the village elders stopped asking about it. It seems that we all can relate to government incompetence and poor quality of service.

What does this story teach us? Humans are so complicated that we have no idea what they will do in any given new situation. We think we do because we are intelligent, but in reality, we are foolish and naïve. We are not one dimensional. We are connected to everyone and everything around us. Any change we make has the potential to affect everything else. The possibility of us making a change in a highly complex system and having it go as we expected is virtually zero. That does not mean we do not change things, but it does mean that we need to acknowledge our lack of understanding and proceed with care.

Begging For Stats

The vast majority of the British public thinks that two parents who are married is the best structure to raise children. Every report I have ever seen says the same thing, but governments do not seem to be pushing it for fear of upsetting particular minority groups. The 2019 report from the *Centre For Social Justice* (https://www.centreforsocialjustice.org.uk/wp-content/uploads/2019/04/CSJJ6900-Family-Report-190405-WEB.pdf) states that 67% of British adults agree with the notion that '*marriage tends to be the most stable environment in which to raise children.*' Yet, 21% of MPs disagreed with the notion that '*the life chances of children with married parents are significantly better than those of children whose parents are not married.*' A fifth of MPs see no benefit for children having married parents – this is surely an example of votes before common sense.

Those who experience family breakdown when aged 18 or younger, are:

- Over twice as likely (2.3 times) to experience homelessness

- Twice as likely (2.0 times) to be in trouble with the police or spend time in prison

- Almost twice as likely (1.9 times) to experience educational underachievement

- Approaching twice as likely (1.8 times) to experience alcoholism

- Approaching twice as likely (1.7 times) to experience teen pregnancy

- Approaching twice as likely (1.7 times) to experience mental health issues

- More likely (1.6 times) to experience debt

- More likely (1.4 times) to experience being on benefits

- Almost twice as likely (1.9 times) to experience not being with the other parent of their children

How do we get the social policy needed if politicians do not think it is important? 83% of British adults say that stronger families are important in addressing Britain's social problems. How does the general public who suffer under poor policy share their knowledge and understanding with politicians?

- 60% of single parents say it is important for children to grow up with both parents.

- 56% of British adults who say that one or more of their children were born out of marriage agree that marriage is the most stable environment in which to raise children.

- 67% of those who are divorced agree that family breakdown is a serious problem in Britain today and more should be done to prevent families from breaking up.

- 89% of British adults who are in their second marriage or more agree that the government is right to say the stability of family matters for children.

- 63% of British adults who are in their second marriage or more agree it is too easy to get a divorce today.

More men than women agree marriage is important and the government should support couples who get married (75% vs 68% respectively). Around half (53%) of British adults agree public money should be spent on strengthening families, while a third (33%) disagree.

In my two decades working mainly with boys and young men, the number one problem I see is the lack of fathers in the home. This is the seed of most of our social issues. The attack on fathers has been progressing since the 1960s thanks to feminism and many other woke progressive movements. But the real damage has been done by governments, not necessarily by design, but definitely by incompetence and unintended consequences.

According to the *Centre For Social Justice* (CSJ) 2018 report (https://www.centreforsocialjustice.org.uk / wp-content/uploads/2018/12/ Testing-Times-FINAL.pdf), birth registration data shows that 95 per cent of births in the UK are to couples. Yet, almost half of all children are no longer living with both their parents by the time they sit their GCSEs. However, for children in our poorest communities, the same proportion has already seen their parents split up by the time they start primary school. An exodus of fathers is taking place and no one seems to notice or care.

An analysis conducted by the CSJ of inspection frameworks related to maternity services, health visitors, and children's centres, found few direct mentions of 'fathers.' For maternity services, the word 'father' is conspicuously absent. The word is being written out of everyday language and is referred to through vague generic terms such as 'birthing partner.'

We seem to be going out of our way to negate the role fathers play in socialising the next generation. When the CSJ asked fathers if they received any guidance on being a father from their health visitor, 44 per cent said that they received 'not a lot' or 'none at all.' We have no official record on how many fathers attend antenatal appointments, as there is no official record of father attendance taken at appointments. Lincolnshire increased the participation rate of fathers in their Primary Birth Visit from 20% to 70%, simply by changing how they addressed new parents in their invitation letter. Instead of addressing the family as *'Dear Parent,'* they wrote *'Dear new Mum and Dad,'* and emphasised their intention of making an *'appointment that is convenient for you both.'*

We have been told that fathers do not take their parenting responsibility seriously and leave the mother to do most of the majority of the work. But *The Modern Families Index* (a major annual survey of working parents) found in 2018 that 46 per cent of fathers either shared childcare duties equally with their partner or did the majority of parenting. Almost half (43 per cent) of younger fathers would be *'happy to take a pay cut if it meant spending more time with their families.'*

Nearly all studies show that high-quality father involvement from the month following birth is associated with a range of positive outcomes, including higher IQs at 12 months and 3 years. When fathers are involved in their children's early lives, children will score higher on measures of cognitive development by the age of five months; by the time they are toddlers they will have better problem-solving abilities, and at the age of three they will have higher IQ scores. School readiness in young children is directly related to the sensitivity and nurturing shown by their fathers in the early years. This trend continues throughout a child's school life.

When we destroy the concept of the family we push people into poverty that delivers poor life outcomes. They then need State support to survive or maintain an acceptable level of existence. They are now beggars, reliant on other people's taxes.

The upsetting realisation is that it does not have to be this way. We never ask people what they want in life, we just see superficial problems and act. We force the poor to drink from the government's water well when they may prefer a nice walk to the river.

A brief history of the welfare state

The *Liberal Party* launched the Welfare State in Britain with a series of major reforms. I was surprised at this fact, I had always thought it was the *Labour Party* – they make you believe it was them.

The Liberal government of 1906–1914 implemented welfare policies concerning three main groups in society: the old, the young and working people.

In 1906 local authorities were allowed to provide free school meals. *The Children and Young Persons Act 1908* was introduced, also known as the *Children's Charter*. This imposed severe punishments for neglecting or treating children cruelly. It was made illegal to sell cigarettes to children or send them out begging. Juvenile courts were set up, which sent children convicted of a crime to borstals, a forerunner of today's youth detention centres.

In 1908 pensions were introduced for the over 70s.

In 1909 *Labour Exchanges* were set up to help unemployed people find work. The *National Insurance Act 1911* was passed, ensuring free medical treatment and sick pay for 26 weeks. An estimated 13 million workers came to be compulsorily covered under this scheme.

The minimum wage was introduced in 1909 for certain low-wage industries and then expanded to include farm labour. The minimum wage only had a short life for a new idea of family allowance targeted at low-income families was introduced to reduce poverty. They were worried about distorting the labour market. This shows that at one point we were capable of thinking about unintended consequences.

After the First World War, the demand for social reform increased, which led to a permanent increase in the role of the State in society. The end of the war also brought an economic slump, particularly in northern industrial towns. This increased with the *Great Depression* of the 1930s. As mentioned earlier in this chapter, for an insight into poverty in northern towns read George Orwell's *The Road To Wigan Pier*.

During the war, the government became much more involved in people's lives, such as the rationing of food, clothing and fuel. Extra milk and meals were given to expectant mothers and children.

The Beveridge Report of 1942, highlighted *Five Giant Evils* in society: squalor, ignorance, want, idleness and disease. It recommended a national, compulsory flat rate insurance scheme that would combine health care, unemployment and retirement benefits. After victory in the 1945 general election, the *Labour Party* pledged to eradicate the giant evils, and undertook measures to provide for the people *'from the cradle to the grave.'*

The experience of almost total state control during the Second World War promoted the idea that a socialist state could solve all social problems. A series of laws were passed such as the *National Assistance*

Act 1948, National Insurance Act 1946, and *National Insurance (Industrial Injuries) Act 1946.*

New policies resulted in an increase in government expenditure and a widening of what was considered to be the State's responsibility, such as increasing redistributive taxation and increasing regulation of industry, food, and housing. The foundation of the *National Health Service* (NHS) in 1948 was a nationalisation process of existing municipal provision and charitable foundations.

Local Politics

This is where I have personally witnessed the most 'political begging.' I worked for a council for nearly a decade and engaged with local councillors and residents daily. Politicians begged for votes, residents begged for priority in services, and at some level, a legal exchange was made. I think this is the definition of politics!

The giver/taker relationship was obvious when it came to the small grants available at the Councillor's discretion – there were checks and balances in place, but these were there for show. Each set of councillors, 3 per voting district, was given a pot of money to be spent on local projects by third sector groups. Active local resident groups knew this and the begging game began.

Powerful community groups would demand a slice of the pie for a specific project. They do not beg for they know they have power when it comes to the reputational damage of a Councillor locally – '*The local park is not safe for your children because the Councillor does not care about you.*' The Councillor knows this is a real possibility so approves the grant and keeps a vocal lobbying group happy and onside. It has been known for Councillors to phone up these groups directly to make sure they know money is available and for them to apply. Local neighbourhoods are run by fiery middle-aged women, do not piss them off – I was scared of a few of them. I am not criticising these ladies, their neighbourhoods were better places to live because of them.

Lesser groups did not receive a phone call. They had to apply for the funding and be judged against other projects, especially if there were more applications than funds available – this is usually the case. How do you ensure your project has the best chance of being funded? Make sure your project fits in with the neighbourhood plan and strategic aims. But it never hurts to suck up to the local councillors by talking positively about them on social media. Or inviting them to your project, and advertising that you will be voting for them at the next election. There is a local election in your neighbourhood 3 times in 4 a year cycle, someone always wants your vote.

Not all councils have grants available to Councillors to award to local groups, but the clever ones do. Especially if controlled by one political party. It makes perfect sense to create dependency within the electorate so other alternatives look like risky options. At one point Manchester had 99% Labour Councillors - someone commented that the difference between Manchester and North Korea was that Manchester had better restaurants. It was a one-party state and still is.

I am not degrading the work of Councillors, I have known some outstanding ones who do sterling work to improve neighbourhoods and the lives of residents. They are normally a local person who still lives in the area, engage with residents daily, and has some understanding of politics. They are the mouthpiece of local people who cannot otherwise be heard.

In 2018, I put my name forward to become a Councillor - an independent candidate for the newly formed *Deansgate Ward* in Manchester city centre. I stood on one issue - rough sleeping. My campaign strap-line was '*voice for the homeless.*' My message was simple. Let us end the epidemic of our fellow citizens living and dying in squalor on the streets. I made it clear I would not work on any other issue while in post. And would not stand again 4 years later, for I did not want to be tempted by the fruits of working within the system. I think I came 7th out of 10 candidates.

The most memorable part of my campaign was an email exchange with a city-centre resident. He asked me what was my stance on more cycle lanes. I replied that I had no stance on this topic for I would only be working on tackling rough sleeping, as this was the city's priority. He replied and thanked me for my honesty, but also informed me he could not vote for me as cycle lanes were his number priority. Bikes over people. His reply shocked me then and still shocks me now on several levels.

During this election, we had approx 200 people sleeping on the streets in the city centre. It was still getting worse. Almost every conversation was about who was to blame, what can be done, and how to fix it. Everyone I spoke to and liaised with online said it was one of their top concerns for Manchester. They did not lie to me, they lied to themselves for they did not really care, they just thought they did. Judge people on their actions, not their words.

There is nothing inherently wrong with an individual making choices based on what is best for them. This is what voting is all about, but should it be? The life of a person living on the street is surely worth more than the personal benefit of a cycle lane. I would be interested if anyone can argue against this proposition. I could have lied, it is easy to do, especially over email. He then may have voted for me but this was not the politician I wanted to be. One lie always leads to another. I was not going to beg for votes – they would come my way if my cause was righteous and my narrative was solid. They did not come. My cause was not righteous. My narrative was not solid. I only have myself to blame for not being a cleverer politician with better communication skills.

Regional Politics

This is a fairly new type of politics in the UK. Starting with devolved powers to different parts of the UK in the 1990s under Tony Blair, and more recently with the introduction of *Police Crime Commissioners* and *Metro Mayors*.

Devolution in Scotland and Wales seems to have caused more problems than they solved. I will leave Northern Ireland out of this for it is too complicated for my ramblings. The idea of a nation is to bring everyone together under a shared concept, but devolution has done the opposite by setting up England as the baddie. Westminster is portrayed as *King John* and only a *Celtic Robin Hood* can get the money back for the people. The truth be told, London and South East subsidise the whole of the UK, we owe this region some gratitude – that is hard for me to say as a Northerner.

The governments of Scotland and Wales are now no better than beggars – not the people for they are amazing. They pretend to be sovereign governments in waiting, but they are not, they are politicians on the hustle. They are selling their constituents a dream of 'freedom' from English tyranny while having their hands stretched out for coin. Recently, the Scottish government stated that the UK must continue to pay Scottish state pensions after independence. Unbelievable.

These governments remind me so much of street beggars. They reject the long term norms that supply the benefits they enjoy because they are selfish and self-centred. They feel victimised and taken advantage of because they are weak and powerless. There is a palpable level of hatred towards their 'so called' abuser – I feel the anti-English hatred when they speak. They constantly take everything on offer, show no gratitude and ask for a greater slice of the pie because they are special and deserving.

My home town of Greater Manchester voted against having a *Metro Mayor* but one was forced upon the people anyway. It was similar to Brexit, except this time the elite got their way. We will let you idiots have a say in your future as long as you give us the answer we want, if not, your voice does not matter. This is probably a discussion for another day.

What has the position of *Metro Mayor* brought to Greater Manchester? After nearly a decade, consisting of two Labour Mayors (Tony Lloyd then Andy Burnham), nothing has improved for the average resident. In fact, I would go further and say the position of Mayor has had a negative impact. It ruined the *Greater Manchester Police* force which is currently in special measures for ignoring 125,000 crimes. It has also led the way for a new regional wide congestion charge on commercial vehicles to supposedly combat air pollution. This was another referendum question the people took part in only to give the wrong answer again – 78% voted against a congestion charge. So the scheme was rebranded as a *Clean Air Zone* and pushed through with no public vote for the plebs cannot be trusted with democracy.

National Politics

This is where most damage to the psyche of the country is done. Governments pander to what the people think they want, instead of what is actually good for them. There is a difference.

Can you remember the last time we solved a national issue? Or when the government took really difficult decisions to tackle an issue of national significance? I do not mean an incident where they threw lots of money at a problem, but sat down and came up with a strategy to solve the problem, regardless of who is upset. You cannot, for I have tried while writing this book and have failed.

The automatic solution to any problem is to assign a budget to it. In the eyes of the public, it looks like it is being tackled and they can stop worrying. It is exactly like throwing a few coins into a paper cup. We know 78p in loose change does not fix any rough sleeper's circumstance, but it makes you feel better and signals to others that you are a good person. The government does this daily on your behalf. They pay guilt money so you think they are virtuous, for this is easier and safer than actually trying to solve the problem. Modern politicians are caretakers, not leaders.

Let us look at three current national tragedies: rough sleeping, knife crime, and rape gangs.

We live in the fifth richest country in the world yet we have fellow citizens living and dying on our streets. How is this allowed? Simple. Rough sleepers do not vote and the people who do vote do not care. To really tackle the issue would require policies that would upset the woke liberal elite, such as a new begging law, hospitalising people who do not accept help, and even prosecuting kind-hearted citizens who hand out money and food. This may affect the way the general public vote after the

Twitterati explodes online. So best not to do anything, make no waves and continue allowing vulnerable people to slowly kill themselves on the streets.

Why do we allow so many young men to die on our streets daily? It is genuinely surprising, especially when the vast majority of them are black. Do black lives matter? We have had two years of everyone saying that they do. The answer to the question is simple. No, they do not matter if the murderer is also black. Who in their right mind would want to try to solve this problem? It is a clear example of where the fear of being accused of racism is actually killing black people. This problem is a poisoned chalice for anyone who attempts to solve it. There are no votes in racism if you are accused of it, so no politician gives it any consideration. *Let them die on the streets next to the homeless.*

The most shocking series of crimes in my life has been the systematic gang rape of thousands of poor white girls. This has taken place in nearly every town and city across the country by predominantly men of Pakistani heritage, but not exclusively. It is still happening and almost every week a new group of men are in court to answer for their crimes. We are talking about tens of thousands of girls, maybe even hundreds of thousands – no one knows for no one wants the answer. Politicians did nothing historically when they were informed and even covered it up for the benefit of 'race relations' – which means votes. Today they still do almost nothing for fear of being accused of racism and losing votes as a consequence. When our politicians are willing to exchange the innocence of our children for votes, then we know they will do anything to stay in power.

During the build-up to general elections, the electorate is most definitely treated as beggars. Every interest group competes against another for some of the national cake as it is sliced. *A reduction in taxes. More money for the NHS. A new law to tackle this or that.* We have months of open bribery as election day gets closer. We do not call it bribery, we call it politics for we are civilised and democratic.

At the last general election in 2019, the *Labour Party* answered a question many people had been pondering for a long time. Can you offer too many bribes to the electorate? And now we have the answer. It is a categorical Yes you can. Jeremy Corbyn offered the country more money for the NHS, an increased minimum wage, pension age freeze, free personal care, net-zero by 2030, nationalise key industries, free bus travel for under-25s, free broadband, and free university. All popular policies individually. But when combined in one bumper package, the electorate realised they were being taken for fools. They knew it could not be delivered or that the country would go bankrupt trying to deliver it. Labour did not have the right narrative, props or ability to pull on the heartstrings. In 2019, they had a poor beggar's narrative for it relied on facts. The winner of this election relied on emotion and pulled the right levers.

Continental Politics

Let us talk about the *European Union*, aka the EU. What could possibly go wrong with such a harmonious conversation?

I shall lay my cards out on the table. I have been a Brexiter all my life, since my middle teens. There was nothing I could have been told that would have made me change my mind and vote to remain in 2016. I am of the opinion that the power to govern our country should be in the hands of the politicians we elect to the *House Of Commons*. To me, the nation-state is sacrosanct.

In my opinion, the biggest issue we had with our previous membership of the EU was that it castrated our politicians in terms of making decisions for our country. We had to accept laws and regulations decided in Brussels, albeit, we had a small say in the making of these rules. We no longer ran our own affairs, we lost control of our destiny, and we started along the path to becoming continental beggars.

Once our politicians realised they had a gold plated excuse not to act on any given topic, they used it. Anything they did not want to do they blamed the EU for tying their hands, all governments did this. The British public started to resent the EU as politicians started to say that they were standing up to it on our behalf. They created a boogie-man. A drama triangle came into play. The UK public was the victim. UK politicians were the heroes. And the EU was the persecutor. Politicians playing this game were where the seed of Brexit was sowed.

After four decades of allowing foreigners to make choices for the UK, we now have an entire political class that does not know how to make difficult decisions. They have never seen any politician do it, it has become a lost art. They do not know how to handle public displeasure when they do what they know is right for the country – they have no one to blame any longer. We have lost conviction in our ability to govern and gained 'focus group' analysis. We no longer have Statesmen or Stateswomen, we have career politicians whose number one priority is to be re-elected. The success of politicians is now measured in years, not in achievement.

I did not personally know anyone who loved the EU before the 2016 referendum was announced. I had only ever heard negative comments about the EU, not many to be fair, but never positive comments. But suddenly the comfort blanket was potentially being taken away and the fear of the unknown came into focus for many people. *'I am a European'* became the new mantra.

One of the hidden traits of our EU membership was the slow manipulation of the British people into European beggars. We would shout with joy when we received 'free' EU money to build a community centre or public work of art. It was marvellous that we were lucky enough to secure such money – pennies from heaven. No one ever mentioned that it was our money. We would send money to the EU as part of our membership and they would send a percentage back to spend on what they ultimately wanted us to spend it on. We also had to put an EU flag on it so everyone would know the money came from our benevolent masters who lived on the continent.

Fear is a powerful motivator. We discovered we had lost confidence in ourselves to govern our own country, make the right choices, and forge our own destiny. This is how many beggars feel when confronted with taking responsibility. They opt to give it away so mistakes cannot be placed on their narrow shoulders. People were afraid of leaving an organisation after 40 years for the country would have to make its own choices. A lack of self-belief in themselves equated to a lack of self-belief in the UK for most Remainers. What if leaving went wrong? Relying on one's self is scary. Far easier to take no chances and keep your hand stretched out like a good beggar.

The Remainer's narrative reached a fever pitch during the EU referendum in 2016. Suddenly, people who had never mentioned the EU before were now discussing all the benefits of membership. *Freedom of movement. Erasmus university scheme. Single market. Customs Union -* which I admit I had never even heard of before. And of course, all the money the EU had spent on the UK. A good beggar can real off all the free stuff that they received, regardless of if any of it was worth having.

Nation Beggars

Countries can be beggars. I do not mean the individuals within them, but the national governments of such countries. Let us look at Africa's post-independence from Western colonial powers. It has been a series of disasters, both natural and man-made. From war, genocide and state oppression, to Ebola, drought and famine. But the biggest disaster in Africa has been its leadership - full of corruption and tribal loyalties. The only success story to come out of Africa has been the Swiss banks and their deposit accounts. Africa has been robbed by Africans. Similar to the trans-Atlantic slave trade, where Africans captured Africans and sold them into slavery for profit.

All my life, Africa has been a beggar. Some people have done very well out of it, some people always do. But many Africans have not seen their lives dramatically improve, they have been continually damaged by their 'so called' leaders with some help from us in the West. Their leaders allowed their countries to be used as pawns during the *Cold War*. They allowed multinationals to harvest their natural resources. They allowed the *World Bank* to dictate the running of their economies. They allowed charities and *Non-Government Organisations* (NGOs) to take care of their people. What did these leaders get in return? More money than you can possibly imagine.

The UK until recently committed 0.7% of its Gross National Product (GDP) to foreign aid, it has now been reduced to 0.5%. The last three years' foreign aid budget amounts: 2021 - £11.1 billion, 2020 - £14.5 billion, 2019 - £15.2 billion. It is a lot of money when you count it in billions.

A lot of this money is wasted for it must be spent in total every year. According to a Daily Mail article in March 2021 (https://www.daily mail.co.uk/news/article-9410357/Britain-blows-millions-taxpayer-funds-foreign-aid-projects.html), we have allocated £700K for 'friendship benches' aimed at encouraging people to discuss their mental health in Zimbabwe. £1 million to 'raise awareness' of the health benefits of brown rice over white rice in Asia. And £1.2 million for an ongoing project to teach children in Bangladesh and Pakistan about the dangers of second-hand smoke. These all may be worthwhile projects, I do not know the details, but are they what the British people think this money should be spent on? I doubt it.

The five poorest countries in the world are the Democratic Republic of Congo, Mozambique, Uganda, Tajikistan and Haiti (these change depending on the year and measuring metric – but my point is still valid). None are in the UK's top 10 beneficiaries.

The countries that receive the most aid are the ones that are the most important to us, such as securing access to their market, or fighting the *'war on terror.'* Half of all international development aid is "tied," meaning that countries must use it to buy goods and services from the donor nation. It is also used as a carrot/stick to ensure countries support regional and international policies beneficial to the donor nation. *No such thing as a free lunch!*

The cost to a country of this type of begging is a loss of control over its future. It becomes a game of *hide & seek*. Time and energy are constantly spent seeking out the next opportunity for international aid so leaders can skim off the top. There is no incentive to solve problems within the country for the aid will stop if successful. If the easy money stops, then the leaders' easy money will also stop.

How about we just send poor countries 'stuff' that they need? Surely this removes corruption and benefits the everyday person. Let us look at second-hand clothes being sent to Africa by Western charities.

I have been to Africa a handful of times, and just like in Asia, you see poor people walking down the street wearing a West Ham football club t-shirt or a Rhino's rugby t-shirt. How on earth are they supporting English sports teams this far away and even purchasing their merchandise? I soon realised that they were not supporters, just purchasers of second-hand clothes from market stalls stocked high with the unwanted clothes of faraway rich people.

I was travelling around Tunisia when I first realised that second-hand clothes were a problem. I was reading a travel guide book that mentioned the filming of the original *Star Wars* film was in Tunisia and discussed the cloaks worn by the *Jawa* - scrap collectors that captured both R2D2 and C3PO on Tatooine. These brown cloaks were based on the traditional local Tunisian coats worn by men. But due to the influx of cheap second-hand garments, including coats, the locals stopped buying them and manufacturers went out of business. Local skilled jobs are gone, replaced with rummaging through piles of old clothes. The next day I started to see the odd old man wearing such a cloak – it made me smile. A giant *Jawa*!

My story is two decades old and during this time the situation has gotten worse for the garment manufacturing trade in African countries. Some countries now have banned or restricted the importation of second-hand clothes to protect local manufacturers and to stop the decline of fashion based cultural expression. Also, the phycological impact of a nation wearing 'cast-offs' from rich white people should not be underestimated.

We cannot always pass a hat around and insist we want to be sovereign, we want to be independent. We should lead and get others to support us, that support will be much more forthcoming when they see how serious and committed we are.
- Kofi Annan, 2016

The law of unintended
consequences is the only real law of history.

- Niall Ferguson

Chapter 6

The Damage

This chapter is the reason why I wanted to write this book, I wanted to highlight the damage. I have seen the unhappy lives of people who were encouraged to make the wrong choices. I have seen the people we have allowed to fail in life. I have seen the misery, the frustration, the anger. I have seen the wasted lives, the untapped potential, and the unfulfilled aspiration.

Life is hard, life is unfair. But nothing is as unfair as failing in life while you have all the tools and opportunities you need to be a success all around you. Failing in a third world country is expected, it is the norm for it is extremely difficult to make change with no access to resources. But failing in the 21st century UK takes a special type of skill, someone has to be trained not to see their mistakes or the opportunities on offer. It is as if we are placing some people on tram tracks heading to '*Loserville*' and they have been told they are in control of the destination. Trams only go where the tracks take them. I would rather people were more uncomfortable and the journey took them longer by relying on themselves to cover the required distance, as long as they arrived at a better destination.

We keep fixing the wrong problems for it is easier than fixing the right ones. We try to fix poverty by handing out money, yet poverty continues. We try to fix education by handing out money, yet 1 in 5 pupils fail school. We try to fix the NHS by handing out money, yet it does not deliver the service we want.

Damaged Individuals

Begging For More

I remember a conversation in a pub several years ago. My friend was telling me about his work colleague who had been diagnosed with cancer and was very ill. They worked for a well known large department store in Manchester.

My friend was critical of their employer. They had informed his friend that they were going to have to terminate his employment for he was not fit to work. They had followed their internal procedure for staff sickness which included full pay for six months, followed by a half pay period. This was all coming to an end which left only dismissal on grounds of ill health. A genuine shame but understandable.

My friend was disgusted. How could a company do this to a sick member of staff? I explained that this company had done more to support his colleague than nearly any other company would ever do. But eventually, the company has to put its future first. It is not a charity or a social welfare project.

He did not understand the point I was trying to make. I knew he had just had a new kitchen fitted at home so I changed my tack. It took a tradesman four days to fit his new kitchen. I asked what would he of done if the tradesman had phoned in sick for the middle two days and therefore needed to work an extra two days to complete the work? Would he have been happy to pay for six days' work? Of course, the answer was No. So where was the difference between this scenario and his friend's case? He could not answer except to say that it is different when it is his money. A very modern socialist answer.

My friend was begging for more, not for himself, but a sick friend. The question is how much free stuff is enough? We need to remember that there is nothing for free, someone has to pay for it. In this case, it is the shoppers at the store who pay a premium so staff can be looked after better than at other stores. When I raised this point my friend understood the logic. He then went on to blow my mind for he told me he never shopped in his store for everything was cheaper elsewhere. I explained he was giving his money to shops that would treat sick staff a lot worse than his employer did. To keep their costs low for customers like him, extra staff benefits would be non-existent. He nodded in agreement. He confirmed he would still use these shops for he needed to be careful with his money. The level of mental gymnastics we perform so we perceive ourselves as moral is spectacular.

Towards the end of the first lockdown during the Covid pandemic, a family member told me she was worried that her child's nursery would not reopen. Or if it did, it may close unexpectedly if a child in their care tested positive for the virus. A lack of child care would cause her huge issues and affect her ability to attend work. A genuine common problem at this time.

She and her husband both worked full time, standard hours and days. They had discussed this potential problem and tried to come up with solutions as a backup. Very sensible. The husband spoke to his boss and asked if this scenario happened could he be furloughed on 80% of his wage – paid for by the government, which is a sneaky way of saying the taxpayer. They were disappointed with the answer. It was No. The company needed all staff working to keep the business going and afloat. Covid had knocked the stuffing out of the business and a fight was now on to save it. The boss was the owner and had his whole life tied up in the company.

The family felt this was very unfair. It would not cost the business a penny, even though it was not meant to be used for such circumstances. It would not be their fault if the nursery closed unexpectedly and their childcare arrangements ended, yet they would be punished by it. They thought the furlough scheme should be changed to allow parents to stay at home to look after their children if needed.

After over a year of the government paying people to stay at home and do nothing, it eventually becomes an expectation and is seen as an entitlement. The more that is given to people, the more that is expected by the people.

Jake was a pleasant man. He would wish everyone a good morning following his request for a few spare coins. It did not matter if people acknowledged him or not when he begged, he still would throw a jolly greeting their way. He was a good beggar. He knew it was a game and he played it well.

He did not sleep on the streets. He had a nice little flat paid for by housing benefits. I remember once chatting with him when his phone rang. It was his landlord, a local housing association. They were informing him that all his repairs had now been logged and a workman would call tomorrow to fit his new kitchen cupboard door. I could not resist a rye smile. The irony was palpable. He was sitting on a street corner actively begging from people walking to work. While at the same time arranging for his landlord to fix the cupboard door under the kitchen sink.

He dressed to look like what he was pretending to be. He placed a rucksack by his side as an advertisement of his social standing – it was full of cardboard to bulk it out, but not to be too heavy to carry. A dirty sleeping bag was laid across his legs. Picture perfect.

He referred to his daily begging routine as his job. He worked 5 days a week. He explained it was hard and it annoyed him when people thought it was easy. He was adamant it was not. He sounded like so many of my friends that were frustrated about the public perception of their job.

I asked him once why he referred to it as his job. Politely I explained he was begging not working. He smiled and corrected me. He told me it was a job. It was an important job. He added to the welfare of society. His job was to make other people feel better about themselves and their lives. If they gave him a few coins they automatically felt better. If they did not and walked on by, they were thankful they were not in the same position and this made them feel better about their life. His job was to spread cheer. He was the homeless Father Christmas, except the giving was the other way around.

It took me many days to process this conversation. It was profound. Not only had he managed to understand how to play the game, but he had worked out the psychological relationship between a beggar and a giver. He understood the game better than anyone I ever met.

Begging To Stay Low

Billy was sitting on the pavement when we first came across him. He was sat crossed legged with his back against the wall of a pub on Deansgate in Manchester city centre. We walked over, introduced ourselves and sat down next to him.

We chatted about his circumstances and asked if we could help him with anything. We explained what we could do and what services were on offer - we laid out his options. It is extremely important for people to have options and to make the choice themselves.

I do not remember how the conversation changed, but I will never forget a statement Billy made. He told us that he was lucky because people treated him better than they do rats. This puzzled us so we asked him to explain. He said that rats have to climb through bins to look for what people do not want and have thrown away. He did not have to do that because people handed him the stuff they did not want. He was better than a rat – that was worth something

He was not trying to make a point or complain. He was explaining his position and where he placed himself in the grand order of things. He classed himself as slightly better than a rat. Not at the very bottom of the value table, which is at least something. *I am Billy. I am better than a rat.* We grasp at small positives when they are the only ones on offer.

How did Billy ever get to such a conclusion? The answer is easy. He saw it with his own eyes. He saw people give him their trash daily. Half-eaten sandwiches, black bananas, bags of crisps from a meal deal, bin bag full of old clothes. Even at homeless shelters, the food is dependent upon donations from takeaways, restaurants and fresh food shops – whatever they cannot sell, they donate. It saves the business money from their commercial waste budget. Did you know that? Shops that give away their unwanted food actually save money in refuge collection fees.

Billy knew he was a beggar. He accepted everything offered to him for that was his role. The vast majority of it would be discarded. Sometimes he would have a choice – day old cheese sandwich or a half-eaten kebab. But he always remembered that he was better than a rat.

A family member explained to me how their boyfriend remains entitled to enhanced disability payments, instead of claiming unemployment benefits. It shocked me then and still does now. The performance, the planning, the deception. I do not remember all the correct information, but the story goes along the lines of this. Every year the boyfriend has to go for an assessment to judge his mental capability and his ability to look after himself. This has been happening for at least a decade. Each assessment confirms that he does not have the capacity to work and needs additional financial support to live at an appropriate level of comfort. This leads to another year with no hassle from the State and regular money guaranteed to hit his bank account. The truth be told, he has no mental capacity issues, it is all a con. He works cash in hand when he feels like it or needs a bit extra, has romantic relationships and socialises when he wants to.

When his annual assessment appointment is a few days away he starts his well-practised routine. No shaving. No washing. No brushing of his teeth. He finds his 'assessment clothes' ready for the appointment. Ill-fitting pants, a faded t-shirt and a 20-year-old shirt with food stains. No item had been washed or ironed for a decade.

On the day of the assessment, he gets into his costume. He does not wash that day. But he does pure a little cooking oil into his palm and rubs it into his hair to give it that greasy – 'never been washed' look. He then combs his hair so he looks very odd. Now he looks and smells the part of a vulnerable socially dysfunctional individual. During the assessment, he acts like someone with low intelligence, poor communication skills, extremely socially awkward and confused. His beggar's narrative is '*a single man who lives alone with no sense of personal hygiene, no personal life and struggles to look after himself.*'

This charade works. Maybe the assessment is actually correct in its findings that he is not mentally competent. You have to be somewhat mentally damaged to carry out such a pretence and degrade yourself in such a manner. How far do you think he would go keep his handouts arriving each month? Soil himself? Cut himself? Accept home-help visits to clean and wash him? We have no idea how far an individual beggar will go – but I do know they can go too far and die from it. The more you portray yourself as weak and vulnerable, the more weak and vulnerable you become. It is a feedback loop that destroys your sense of self, it eats you from the inside out.

Begging For Snow

Snowflakes. We have all heard this term directed at young people who seem not to be able to cope with modern life. They need and demand safe spaces for protection, and trigger warnings to survive interactions, and they become upset with perceived micro-aggressions. They label almost everything they dislike as hate speech or fascism. They see injustice everywhere which causes them distress and pain. The term snowflake mocks their special uniqueness and highlights their extreme delicateness - destruction with a single touch.

How did we create such pathetic weaklings? It cannot be their genes for their recent ancestors stormed the beaches in Normandy during the D-Day landings. It has to be an effect of nurture: parental, societal and peer group.

Snowflakes tend to be middle-class with a good education. An upbringing where everything was provided in abundance and the environment had been artificially sanitised to be free of danger and issues. 'Spoilt' – is what we use to call them.

Today, they arrive at university and real life hits them straight in the face. Life is messy, unsafe, complicated and demanding. How did other generations cope? I do not know how, they just did. It is called growing up and taking responsibility. Something new must be present that will not allow these individuals to progress to maturity.

This missing piece of the puzzle is called 'smartphones.' Social media is life, especially for the young. It connects them to all their friends, keeps them in the loop and offers them their opinion on many topics. It is a tool, a deity, a friend and a dictator. It is a life support machine -

existence is worthless without it.

As a young person, you have witnessed individuals attacked and mauled online, just for expressing a view, having an opinion or cracking a joke. You are aware that last month's opinions may not be permissible today. You have no understanding of how or why these things change, but you know they do, for you read about it online.

You know everything you ever say online is there forever - a scary fact. The fear of ruining your life with a tweet before it has even begun must be tremendous. You start to publicly censor your opinions and views. You go along with ideas that you disagreed with to cause no waves – over time you find yourself agreeing with them either through fear or repetition. You follow the crowd. You take a knee, post a black square and flagellate yourself for having privilege. You put your pronouns in your bio without understanding why. Every month you search out the latest trendy flag to fly next to your avatar on social media. It is mentally exhausting.

You exist but you are not alive. You navigate the culture war minefield and avoid the sneaky booby-traps. You try to control your surroundings and the information you are exposed to so you do not make a mistake. Your fundamental beliefs are challenged - you are tested by others. Will you pass the test and repeat the mantra? *Trans women are real women.* Will you judge people based on their skin colour and not on their character? *Black Lives Matter.* All you now see is race, gender and sexuality.

The universities are not helping the matter by infantilising students and creating dependency. This is not because the universities care, but because they are now businesses and each student is worth £9000 a year. To ensure they keep every single golden goose, they go out of their way to indulge any silly request if the majority of the student body supports it. The customer is always right – except in this matter. Universities continue to make a huge fundamental mistake in their thinking, students are not customers, they are the product. If the product becomes less valuable then fewer people will want it, therefore the price that can be asked for it reduces.

Whilst in the middle of this roller-coaster, you begin to doubt if you are still a good person. You are conscious that you are acting contrary to what you believe to be right and moral. Facts you knew were true and solid are now false, fluid or malleable. *Down is up. Left is right.* People argue that 2+2=5 and they are not joking. You hide your true self for fear of criticism and destruction. You trust no one, for no one can be trusted.

Your tutors are cowards at best or far-left propagandists who promote this new warped ideology. Your parents have no concept of the modern world and cannot help, so you do not ask. You have no one you can trust or speak to, for Judas could be around any corner. You have to figure it out by yourself. You are petrified.

Imagine the above is your life at 20 years old, how would you cope? How long before a decline in your mental health, your self-esteem, your confidence. Even your belief system of right and wrong is damaged. How do you stop the pain, the confusion and the distress?

Maybe an answer is to remove yourself from all situations that trigger your anxiety. To avoid conversations that make you question your thoughts and beliefs. To run to a safe space where reality and dogma do not meet. A place where you can gain some control over your mental state, and then continue with the rest of your day without crumbling.

When you have not been exposed to the real world it is overwhelming when you finally realise it is a dangerous place. When you have been taken care of so completely you do not know how to deal with conflict, danger or evil. When everything has been handed to you on a silver platter, you have no concept of how to strategise to get what you need.

We have definitely created a generation of weaklings who cannot stick up for themselves and have been damaged through mass online hypnosis. Fear of the unknown, fear of being unpopular, fear of excommunication from the group. No ability to speak the truth or live by the morality of their upbringing. Potentially a generation of cowards who would rather live as slaves and beggars, than take the path of righteousness and responsibility.

It's better to die free than live as a slave. - **Frederick Douglass**

Or, are they just children bombarded with information, opinions and views on an hourly basis. Trying to make the best decisions based on their limited life experience, with no one to ask for help or advice. Compounded by no opportunity to discuss or debate ideas for they have all been closed down and are forbidden. *"That's hate speech! You fucking Nazi."*

A generation spoilt by society, expecting life to be easy. Have we let them down?

Begging For Bollywood

The film *Slumdog Millionaire* tells the story of Jamal, a boy who lives in the slums of Mumbai. He ends up on the Indian version of the TV game show *Who Wants To Be A Millionaire?* One of the most disturbing scenes in the film is where a small homeless boy is encouraged to sing aloud, his voice is beautiful. He is picked as a winner and is jubilant as he is led away, held down and blinded by having hot oil droplets placed into his eyes. He is now a perfect beggar. Deformed with the voice of an angel – a money-making machine.

This scene was not an evil invented fantasy, but an everyday occurrence in India where the begging trade is huge and very profitable. In January 2009, the *Daily Mail* did a piece on the real *Slumdog Millionaires* and the mafia crippling kids for profit (https://www.daily mail.co.uk/news/article-1127056/The-real-Slumdog-Millionaires-Behind -cinema-fantasy-mafia-gangs-deliberately-crippling-children-profit.html). They highlighted several real personal experiences of kids tricked and then enslaved into the trade. One 12-year-old boy fled his drunken father in rural India, he sneaked onto a train bound for the city. A nice couple said they could help and gave him cakes. When he woke up he was in a hospital missing a leg. He was rescued from the hospital by a charity. Another boy was 15 years old when he was tricked to go to another city for a better life. They took away his leg and brought him straight back to Mumbai to work as a beggar. According to official figures, as many as 44,000 children fall into the clutches of the beggar mafia in India each year and of these, hundreds are deliberately mutilated.

A story in the *New York Times* (https://www.nytimes.com/2006/08/03/world/asia/03iht-letter.2379071.html) from 2006 exposed three Indian doctors, who were caught by a hidden camera agreeing to amputate the healthy limbs of beggars to increase their takings. One of the doctors makes a promise to the undercover journalist: "*Believe me, if there are two beggars in front of you and one of them is lame, you will give the money to the lame beggar.*"

If a child fights back and refuses to go along with the mutilation the outcome is much worse (https://www.dailymail.co.uk/news/article-2244533/Mutilated-gang-set-maim-hed-earn-beggar-seven-year-old-boy-story-common-Bangladesh.html). A seven-year-old boy in Bangladesh was grabbed from the street to be maimed so he would elicit more sympathy working for them as a beggar. But when he recognised the men and told them he would report them to his father, they decided to torture him, cutting off his penis and leaving him for dead on the streets of Bangladesh. He survived.

Damaged Families

People damages families. The State damages families. Families damage themselves. When we allow families to be damaged, they go on to damage communities and society. I have spent decades working with such families.

It is amazing that we still have the 'family unit' left in the UK considering the sixty-year onslaught against it from governments, feminists and progressive lefties. Family is the most important social structure we have. It is the base of community and society. It is in our DNA - seeking out our ancestors is a multi-million-pound industry. We would not have this innate desire if it was not important. But the family unit can be damaged and even broken.

The breakdown of the nuclear family and acceptance of single parenthood has had huge negative effects on children. A government report from March 2021 (https://www.gov.uk/government/statistics/ children-living-with-parents-in-emotional-distress-march-2021-update/ statistical - commentary - children - living - with - parents - in - emotional- distress-march-2021-update) looked at children reporting emotional distress to see if the parents' living arrangements were a factor. It found that 1 in 3 children lived with at least one parent – this measure included children living with one or both parents. But around 1 in 22 children lived with both parents – these children were more likely to report emotional distress if both parents were out of work. Having both parents living with you as a child makes you happier. But are there more benefits if your parents are married, as opposed to just cohabiting

A report from 2018 by the *Institute For Family Studies*, (https://if studies.org / blog /the-long-term-benefits-of-marriage-evidence-from-the-uk) found that regardless of family and social background, those born to married parents were 23% more likely to have been to university, 10% more likely to have got married themselves, and 16% less likely ever to have received government benefits. Married parents have a big impact on the future lives of their children, yet money appears to play no role whatsoever.

We all know the above is true, we feel it in our gut. That is why we have spent hundreds, if not thousands of years promoting such arrangements, writing them into our holy books, and shaming people who transgressed for we had their best interests at heart. But over the last half-century, we have developed social policies that have attacked the family by removing fathers in exchange for State handouts and disincentivising marriage by giving cohabitation the same value. A marriage contract is the only legal contract in the UK where you can break it with no penalty – legally speaking. It is now just a worthless piece of paper. It is a letter to Father Christmas or a Valentine's Day card. A contract between two people must mean something if it is to be valued.

If we can damage a family enough then the effects can be passed down generationally. The intergenerational earning potential of UK families is low compared to other countries. This means if you are born poor, you have a greater risk of staying poor compared to other OECD (*Organisation for Economic Co-operation and Development*) countries.

A government report, (https://webarchive.nationalarchives.gov. uk/ukgwa / 20160105214416 / http://www.ons.gov.uk/ons/rel/household-income/intergenerational-transmission-of-poverty-in-the-uk---eu / 2014/ blank.html), looking at the intergenerational transmissions of poverty identified the childhood factors that matter the most.

Educational attainment has the largest impact on the likelihood of being in poverty. Those with a low level of educational attainment are almost five times as likely to be in poverty now and 11 times as likely to be severely materially deprived as those with a high level of education. Growing up in a workless household also appears to have an impact on future poverty. Those who lived in a workless household at age 14 are around 1.5 times as likely to be in poverty compared with those where one adult was working. The father's level of education has the largest impact on the likelihood of low educational attainment. People are 7.5 times more likely to have a low educational outcome themselves if their father had a low level. People are around 3 times more likely to have a low educational outcome if their mother has a low level of education. There is also a relationship between people's educational outcomes, the number of adults and children living in the household, and the employment status of the parents.

Of those studied, educational attainment is the most important factor in explaining poverty in the UK. Those with a low level of educational attainment are almost five times as likely to be in poverty now as those with a high level of education. The financial situation of the household as a child is not a significant predictor of childhood poverty. This suggests that household income during childhood mainly impacts future life chances through the educational attainment of the child.

It is clear from this report that we cannot buy people out of poverty, we must educate them out of it. We must stop children today from failing eleven years of state-funded education. Failing not only damages their life outcomes, but also damages their future children's life chances. A failed education means begging off the State which is then seen as normal by children in the household, who grow up to beg off the State themselves.

This is how families are damaged, we strip away their power to make decisions that would improve them as a unit, and we make them answerable to the State. And for some, we make them dependent upon the State and other charitable organisations. This is more acceptable than allowing a small minority to fail which may generate a negative Press headline. How can we expect people to learn from their mistakes and improve their lives when we never allow them to fail.

Begging For Family

Families can be the invisible victim, they are silent for they are forgotten or ignored. No one ever talks to the family of a beggar. At some level, we blame them for abandoning a vulnerable family member to live on the streets. The family should have tried harder, for longer, and been more persistent. People have said to me that if their family member was a druggie living on the streets, they would kidnap them and keep them imprisoned until they were clean of drugs. A crazy solution to a problem they have no understanding of.

The vast majority of families love their relatives. They would have tried everything to help but to no avail. The end of the relationship comes after many incidents of theft, open drug use, arguments, and trouble knocking on the door. The family eventually gives up. It is understandable. But the love does not stop for you cannot stop loving your son, daughter, uncle, or parent.

In some cases, the family have no idea where their family member is or the lifestyle that has been chosen. During a visit to the Northern Quarter of Manchester city centre, my team saw a new face and sat down on the street to introduce themselves and have a chat. He was a chronic drug addict and had recently turned up in Manchester. The city has a national reputation within homeless circles as the place to go to be a rough sleeper. So proud that my city has such a wonderful reputation!

He was originally from Portsmouth but had not been home for several years. He said he had pleasant memories of home but it was mixing with the wrong people that had ruined his life. He suddenly started to go through his pockets as if looking for something important. He pulled out a £2 coin, quite rare. Not expensive rare, but rare enough that when you get one you look at it before putting it in your pocket.

He held it in his fingers as he told us about his sister and her child, his niece. When he lived at home he use to save every £2 coin he got and give it to his niece for her savings. He told us he had had many in the last two years and each one makes him think of her and how much she must have grown. A tear appeared. He asked us would we send her the coin and say it was from her uncle? He admitted that the coin would not see the end of the day if left with him. Like all the others he had possessed in the last few years, he would spend it on drugs, instead of giving it to the child he loved. We could not refuse. We wrote down the address he gave us and posted the coin later the same day.

The next morning, we received a phone call. It was his mother. She had received the letter and coin. She explained that she had not heard from her son in two years and had no idea if he was dead or alive. Imagine her constantly wondering what had become of her son? Was it her fault? Was he staying away because of her? Was she a bad mother?

She was so thankful to us for writing and letting her know about him. The coin was already in the child's piggy bank. She then asked us for a favour. *Would we meet her later that day in Manchester city centre for she was already in her car driving north?* She wanted to speak to her son and bring him home.

We met her in a car park in the city centre and started the search for her son. It was easier than we imagined. We found him in exactly the same spot as the day before. The tears flowed. She held him so tight, for so long – the smell and grime did not phase her. A mother's love. We walked them both back to the car and she took him home where he belonged. Result.

I remember working on community engagement days while at a council. These were events where we would set up stalls and hand out information on different services. We would ask a few people to fill in questionnaires so we could say we had consulted the community on our plans for their neighbourhood. Almost a complete waste of time, except for the fun stuff we would put on for the kids.

To make people turn up we would have to put on a buffet or even a 'hot pot' with pickled red cabbage. Every stall would have freebies, such as keyrings, pens and mouse mats. As time went on, budgets increased. Freebies included pen drives, food vouchers, window alarms and smoke detectors.

Over a decade, we had taught local people that council events meant free stuff. Whole families would turn up and clear whole tables by themselves. Parents, kids, aunties and grandparents would take everything on offer, and more. I had to stop people on several occasions from taking our plastic storage boxes and folding chairs. These families acted like locus. It happened in all communities but the Roma were the gold medallists.

It was learnt behaviour, it was cultural. It was what parents taught their kids based on their experience of life in a society that handed out free stuff. Take anything on offer, take it all. We can decide later if we want it.

If this is the message to kids of primary school age, how do we expect them to be different when they grow up and have their own families. Intergenerational lack of shame. A mindset that says take, take and then take some more.

Food banks are a good example of this take & take lifestyle from specific families. Some people will genuinely fall upon hard times and need some assistance. How much of this could have been prevented by the individual is another question. But poverty does not explain the growth in foodbank use in the UK.

If I was standing in the middle of a high street handing out £10 notes, I would soon run out of money. This does not mean that the local area is full of people with no money. It just means that when you give away items that people want, people will take them. My mum gets given a food hamper every Christmas by the local community association just because she is old. She accepts but she does not need it.

After decades of training families to accept handouts with no sense of shame, we should not be surprised when they do. Saving £5 a week on your shopping bill by using a food bank means you have £5 extra to spend on something else. Common sense.

We need to instil the mindset I had when I was a child queuing up outside the school office to receive my 5 weekly free dinner tickets. I was not embarrassed to receive them, but I knew my child would never be stood in such a line. Accept charity when needed, but train your children not to need it and they will not have to accept it.

Damaged Community

We may only see the pathetic faces of dishevelled individuals as we throw a few coins into their paper cups. But do you understand the real danger the beggar has placed themselves in? They risk being assaulted and robbed just to allow you to feel wonderful, as your copper coins hit existing pennies in the bottom of the paper cup.

Have you ever heard of 'push' and 'pull' factors in terms of social issues?

A push factor is an external influence that has the effect of pushing you away from something. Loneliness may 'push you' to spend as much time as possible out of your home. Poor mental health may 'push you' to make poor choices. Disliking your family may 'push you' to avoid them when help is needed.

A pull factor is the opposite of a push factor. These are the external influences that have the effect of pulling you towards something. Free money from begging may 'pull you' to the streets. Easy access to cheap drugs may 'pull you' to the city centre. Having people to speak to may 'pull you' to hang out all day with other broken individuals.

Beggars have many push factors in their lives that contribute to their decision-making process. Their lives are chaotic, painful and disappointing. Poor mental health developed over a lifetime is compounded by drug addiction, poor physical health, lack of sleep and genuine fear.

Pull factors for beggars are easily identified. Let us start with the obvious. Free money - everyone would like free money, I would. But we have a longer list than just free money. Free food - this is almost as good as free money for it saves you spending your own money and keeps you in the city centre longer. Social interaction - we are social creatures and crave interaction with others. Sense of purpose - we need a purpose in life, a reason to get out of bed in the morning, otherwise, the void slowly destroys us. Instant gratification – every coin, every sandwich received is a small reward and a validation. Humans are complicated creatures.

Begging For A Smack

One of the negative effects of being pulled into the city centre is the high level of violence within the homeless community. Broken individuals socialising in the city centre is called *Street Life* - not all are homeless, some are just day visitors. Violence in this community is akin to *Lord Of The Flies* - only the strong survive. Violence is an everyday occurrence. It is expected. It is guaranteed. Therefore, some individuals are primed to be aggressive at any moment, especially if they feel threatened. A couple of years ago it was common for beggars and rough sleepers to carry squeezy bottles full of bleach as a defensive weapon. Similar to a spitting cobra, the target would be the eyes so a hasty retreat could be made. People keep their distance from cobras. They may get a warning and if not heeded, they get a face full of venom. Other individuals carry knives, screwdrivers and other weapons. To overcome the risk of *Stop & Search* by the police, many hide their weapons close by. In bushes, in litter bins or in the pocket of someone much weaker and easily intimidated into compliance. Being armed within two seconds is an acceptable amount of time to wait. It was such a problem that Manchester council proactively cut down all bushes and flower beds in the notorious Piccadilly Gardens in an attempt to remove hiding places for weapons. While this horticultural exercise was taking place, it coincided with a heavy police presence. Council gardeners insisted on the police presence, they were not going to uncover and remove weapons without backup standing next to them. Very sensible.

Local newspaper headlines for Manchester city centre:

"A homeless man was screaming" - *Two stabbed and two others injured during Piccadilly Gardens violence* - 12th January 2020

Band of homeless people attacked innocent man in city centre during 'spice rage' when he tried to save his girlfriend from them - 17th September 2020

Homeless man left naked in the street after being robbed of everything - 3rd December 2020

Couple who battered and stabbed a homeless man they accused of stealing a handbag as he lay stuck in his sleeping bag are jailed for 12 years - 12th March 2019

Homeless man sexually attacked unconscious woman on Piccadilly Gardens bench - 20th May 2021

I could print pages of these headlines for Manchester city centre, especially focusing on Piccadilly Gardens. By creating pull factors for the city centre and encouraging vulnerable and damaged individuals to socialise together in one place, we have created an open-air lunatic asylum. But with no nurses. These day-patients sometimes try to kill each other, while at the same time their lifestyle is slowly killing them all.

Piccadilly Gardens is right in the heart of Manchester city centre. It would not be out of place in the city of San Francisco – a drug-ridden, crime-infested, open-air lunatic asylum. We should we rename my city to *Man Franchester*. Progressive policies are enabling damaged individuals to create their own living hell on earth. The city is getting worse yet the people keep voting for the same local politicians with the same ideas. Have a look on YouTube to see what San Francisco is like today. This is what our cities will become if we carry on down this path of *'rights with no responsibility.'*

In 2018, I met a victim of one of these terrible violent episodes. He may have been a victim but he was not an innocent victim. Let's call him Mick. He had an Irish accent and I seem to remember he was part of the travelling community. He was not homeless. He was a clean-shaven well presented young man. Built like a barn door and could handle himself. One of my outreach workers introduced me to him in Piccadilly Gardens. He had become a bit of an overnight celebrity. People wanted to see the 12-inch scar on his face. From the tip of his chin to his right ear. A smooth clean cut. Stitches removed but still obviously a very new injury. It was five weeks old. He told me the story with glee. He had been drinking all day in the Gardens. He was a drinker, not a druggie. Drinking was acceptable and normal in his opinion. Drugs were a different kettle of fish of which he disapproved. He got involved in an argument with a little Eastern European homeless fellow. There was no explanation of why. Mick had found the confrontation amusing. He used his size to intimidate the smaller fellow and sent him on his way with a warning of forthcoming violence if he did not *fuck-off*. Large physically powerful men have a habit of pissing off others. They tend not to know about it for they are large physically powerful men. But this little Eastern European was not made of the same stuff as other people. His countrymen and ancestors were not accustomed to an easy life and would not accept an insult without retribution. When Mick had turned his back, the offended man came back with a knife and jumped on Mick's back. He placed his knife across Mick's throat and pulled back hard. Luckily for Mick, he had tried to buck the little man off his back and in doing so had lowered his head. This placed his chin on his chest and protected his neck. The slice was meant to cut his throat. Instead, it sliced his chin, cheek and ear. I do not see how he would have survived this damage had it been accurately delivered. I asked about the assassin and if he had been arrested. The answer was No. Which was exactly what Mick said he wanted. Mick was not helping with the police enquiries. He openly told me he was going to find the man, kill him and take the body to the moors to bury.

No one ever saw the Eastern European man again. Was he taken on a trip to the moors? If this would have happened then everyone would have been talking about it – the word on the street was that he left Manchester to be homeless somewhere else. Exactly what I would do if the police were looking for me and I was living on the streets. And let us not forget a huge Irish monster with fists the size of shovels hoping for a surprise reunion.

When we have people making money, we always have counterfeiters, pirates, robbers and protection rackets. It has been the same throughout history and it is the same in Manchester city centre today regarding the begging trade. Do not be fooled, it is a trade. Donations are swapped for drugs several times a day. The amount of money passing hands is tremendous. Pre-Covid we estimated that an average beggar would earn £100 per day and also be on full benefits. A vulnerable looking teenage girl could earn £300 to £400 per day. A good beggar will not tell you the truth for it may stop future donations if the scam is highlighted. Poor beggars will not tell you the truth for they do not want you to judge them in comparison to the good beggars. And as I have said several times, *'never believe a word a beggar says!'*

Weak and vulnerable people need protection, they always have. We have spoken to many rough sleepers who had been robbed during the night. Sometimes by stealth, usually their shoes or other items, but also their money and drugs. This happens by usually more than one attacker, they sit on the victim and search everywhere on their victim, and I mean everywhere. The number of blows you encounter depends on how hard you struggle. The day after such a beating is a good day to discuss their options of getting off the street. We have found we have helped more people after such an incident than any other time. Their fear at this moment is greater than their need for drugs. After a few days, it is history and forgotten about.

Assaults are an everyday occurrence in such a chaotic community. Arguments arise over everything and nothing. But usually over money and drugs. Not paying back a debt, not sharing a score, not splitting donations. A slap may be encountered if you are sitting in another beggar's spot – territorial disputes can escalate quickly into stabbings.

Other incidents are just so crazy that you could not make them up if you tried. A sad case was of Daniel Smith who my staff knew. I did not. He was living in a tent under a bridge in the city centre when he was beaten to death and set on fire in January 2016. A dispute had occurred among a group of rough sleepers where Daniel, in a drunken and drug-induced stupor, urinated on someone else's belongings. Two men were found guilty and received sentences of over 20 years each.

This case shows what happens when we leave mentally ill individuals to live on the streets and the general public enables them to reject the support on offer by handing over money for drugs and food. Society should have been on trial that day in court for we allowed it to happen. We do not complain to our MPs, we do not organise marches, we do not take the knee in solidarity. We do nothing for deep down inside we do not really care. Hard to hear, but all the evidence shows it to be true.

Begging For A Bargain

When we promote greed and pit one another against each other it does not end well. This can be said of the American ritual of *Black Friday*. It is the first Friday after Thanksgiving and is considered the first day of the Christmas shopping period. Luckily for us, it has not taken off in the UK.

In America, it is an annual tradition of bad manners, selfishness, disrespect and violence. According to the *New York Times* in November 2020, an article with the title: *Black Friday's most gruesome injuries and deaths through the years*, stated that *"between 2006 and 2018, 44 Black Friday incidents in America left 11 dead and 109 injured."* Ho-ho-ho. Peace on earth.

All this carnage to buy presents during the Christian festive period that pretends to promote '*goodwill to all men.*' But when we allow a lack of shame to run free, combined with greed, people only see the world through their desires and wants. A world where they are the most important person, where life is a game to be won, and you do not care about others. *Dog eat dog.*

Damaged Society

Begging does not only damage individuals, it also damages wider society by having less productive citizens who require more State intervention. More people taking out, fewer people putting in. More tax-eaters, fewer taxpayers. We spend approx £100 billion a year on benefits for working-age people in 1.8 million households. That's £1 in every £8 the government spends.

What could we do to improve society if we had £100 billion extra every year? Let us put this number in perspective. In 2019/20, we spent: NHS £166B, Education £103B, Defence £52B. If we could reduce the number of people unemployed or underpaid, then we would have the extra benefit of increased taxes paid by these people. I am not saying we can get rid of the whole of the £100B, or even most of it. But my point is that unproductive citizens are a drain on society. We need to be ensuring that we stop producing so many after eleven years of state-funded education.

Begging To Be Accepted

The fat acceptance movement is a social movement to eliminate the social stigma of obesity. It can be dated back to 1967 when 500 people met in New York's Central Park to protest against anti-fat bias. As with most protest movements from the 60s onwards, they needed to destroy something, so they set on fire a selection of diet books as a sign of their rejection of the social norm of healthy body shape.

Once full female equality was gained in the 1970s and written into law, the feminist movement appropriated the fat movement. In 1979, a new phrase was coined '*Big Beautiful Woman*' which captured the hearts of fat women everywhere. While at the same time removing a little of their personal responsibility.

Over the last few decades, this movement has been welcomed into the social justice movement as obesity is now supposedly linked to race, class and sex. It is also heavily influenced by *Queer Theory* – a critical theory that sees all social norms as problematic. A new academic area of research and scholarship has been developed to study and validate this movement, it is called *Fat Studies*. It sits alongside *Black Studies, Gender Studies,* and *Queer Studies*. All a 'waste of time' Studies.

In the UK, you are more likely to be obese if you are black so this is seen as systematic racism. (https://www.ethnicity-facts-figures.service.

gov.uk/health/diet-and-exercise/overweight-adults/latest) Men are more likely to be overweight, but women are more likely to be obese which is proof that the patriarchy is oppressing women. (https://digital.nhs.uk/data-and-information/publications/statistical/statistics-on-obesity-physical-activity-and-diet/statistics-on-obesity-physical-activity-and-diet-england-2019/part-3-adult-obesity) Class is just another word for poverty - poorer people, especially their children, have the highest rate of obesity which is surprising considering they have the least money to spend. (https://www.gov.uk / government / publications / childhood-obesity-applying-all-our-health/childhood-obesity-applying-all-our-health)

A 2017 government report (https://www.gov.uk/government/publications / health-matters-obesity-and-the-food-environment / health-matters-obesity-and-the-food-environment--2) highlights obesity as an increased risk of developing a whole host of diseases. Increased risk of certain cancers, including being 3 times more likely to develop colon cancer. More than 2.5 times more likely to develop high blood pressure - a risk factor for heart disease. Five times more likely to develop type 2 diabetes. It is estimated that the NHS spent £6.1 billion on overweight and obesity-related ill-health from 2014 to 2015. This is projected to reach £9.7 billion by 2050, with wider costs to society estimated to reach £49.9 billion per year.

An all-party UK parliamentary group published a report in 2012 called *Reflections on Body Image*, which found that 1 in 5 British people had perceived to have been victimised because of their weight. The report recommended that *Members of Parliament* investigate putting *"appearance-based discrimination"* under the same legal basis as sexual or racial discrimination by changing the *Equality Act 2010* which makes it illegal to harass, victimise or discriminate against anyone based on specific characteristics.

Why are we, as a society, constantly putting 'feelings' over 'facts?' A fat person may be upset and embarrassed for being obese. But pandering to their feelings does not help them avoid life-threatening illnesses and life of depression. Fat people know they are fat. Not one of them is happy about the fact, regardless of what they tell you. We have all seen fat actresses and fat celebrities promote fat acceptance during interviews and been applauded for it. But when they decide to lose weight, they tell us all how amazing they feel and are so happy. UK Singer Adele. Actresses Rebel Wilson, Gabourey Sidibe, Ricki Lake, Melissa McCarthy. All pretended to be happy and in control when they were fat, but the truth came out after weight loss. I am not saying that losing weight is easy, it is not. But saying being fat is healthy and desirable is perverse.

I can't stop eating. I eat because I'm unhappy, and I'm unhappy because I eat. It's a vicious cycle. **- a quote from a badly named character in the second Austin Powers film.**

The above is the cycle I see many people trapped in. I have family members in this position. I watch their mental and physical health decline as they dampen down their internal pain with food. This increases their unhappiness, so more food is required to reduce the pain again. Poor physical health then makes physical activity more difficult so less exercise is taken, which compounds weight gain and depression.

Like a beggar on a street corner craving a fix, once they get it they damage themselves slight more. Over time, they need a higher quantity of drugs to push the increasing pain away. This damages them even deeper and so requires more drugs to tackle. You have a huge problem when your medicine is the illness.

Being conscious of your own weakness and watching it ruin your life must damage you mentally. The feeling of helplessness, the feeling of disgust at yourself. The crumbling confidence and self-respect. A living hell. But pretending you do not have a problem, and encouraging the world to pretend as well, does not change reality. It just allows more damage to be done.

Begging To Be Adored

Marcus Rashford is a young English man from my city. He plays football at the world-famous *Manchester United Football Club*. He has no financial worries, but this was not always the case.

A couple of years ago, he started a campaign to force the government to feed children during the summer school holidays. It got national attention and the government eventually conceded. Marcus who is a multi-millionaire became the hero of the invisible starving children. This made him a celebrity outside of footballing circles and earned him an MBE – just like me.

Marcus is probably a very nice young man and has the best intentions. Who could be against feeding children? Me, for one! It is the responsibility of the parents to look after and feed their children, not the State. Marcus did not raise the money needed or put his hand in his deep pockets. No. He forced the government to do it with negative Press headlines. Remember that government money means taxpayers' money. Other people across the country had to pay for free food to be delivered to the children of parents who lack responsibility. At the same time, these same taxpayers are also funding government-run projects to combat obesity in some of the same children. It makes no sense.

Marcus' selling point as an individual was that he was poor as a kid and came from a single-parent household - just like millions of other kids. He has told stories of going to bed hungry. I do not believe these stories, but let us say they are true. Who is at fault for a kid going to bed hungry? This answer is easy. Mum and Dad. His mum was a single parent so obviously a Saint and pure of heart. His dad was missing in action.

He would never have found himself in this situation if his mum had been more choosy in picking a potential father for her children. It would have also been beneficial if his dad had been a real man and not abandoned his family. The responsibility lies with both parents. No one else.

Why I am bringing up this young man? It is not to criticise him personally, he is doing something he thinks is beneficial. Something the majority of people in the country think is a good idea. But it has negative consequences. It creates more State dependency and allows parents to be beggars, instead of the leader of their families.

In 2018/19, the percentage of UK children who were overweight or obese in Year 6 was 34.3%, it was 22.6% for kids in Nursery. Kids are getting fatter, and have been for a long time, not slowly starving to death. Surprisingly, it is not the rich kids with money getting fat. The poorer you are, the more chance you overeat and become obese. This seems counter-intuitive, but poorer kids are approx 2.5 times more likely than rich kids to be overweight. See report for more details: https://www.gov.uk/government / publications / childhood - obesity - applying - all-our-health/childhood-obesity-applying-all-our-health

How can we have a section of poor kids potentially killing themselves from overeating, while at the same time, have kids on the same street going hungry because parents have no money to buy food? It does not make any sense. If we had children turning up at hospitals malnourished we would all know about it – it would be all over the TV. The only thing I have seen on TV is the usual obese parent saying how they have to miss meals to ensure their child does not. If someone has to miss a meal then it should be the parent, but in many cases, I do not believe the parent has ever missed a meal.

What we have here is an example of what happens when you turn people into beggars and ask them if they would like some more free stuff. The answer is always Yes. Of course, many parents will accept free food if offered. They would be mad to refuse for saving a little money is always sensible.

Please, sir, I want some more. - **Oliver Twist**

These types of policies take away the responsibility of parents. We have spent half a century undermining the family. We have kicked the father out of the home, and now we want to remove parental responsibility for feeding their own children. The answer should never be that the State must step in and be a parent.

What is the next responsibility we take away from parents? Dressing their child in the morning? Making sure children wash and are clean? Administering proscribed medicine? The child belongs to the parent or it does not. We cannot keep doing this pink and fluffy nonsense of stepping in, taking over, and degrading the role of the parent. The only time we should step in is when the child is at serious risk of death.

Children are being brought up today, just like Marcus, thinking that the State is the boss of their family and children. That anytime something is needed then the State must provide it. It can never be the parents' fault for making poor choices, picking inadequate partners or abandoning their family. We need to stop teaching the next generation that parenthood is just an extension of the State.

A couple of decades ago when I worked for a council, I was dealing with a local *smackhead* who was causing problems for residents. We were looking at obtaining a court order to control where he was allowed to visit – he was a pain.

I mention him not to discuss his behaviour but to highlight how a broken system keeps people in the mode of a beggar. This particular 'waste of space' had a baby boy being brought up by grandparents. The child had a skin condition and needed cream applied every day. The father was the baby's registered carer for this condition but had never once touched the cream. But he did touch the extra monthly payment that arrived in his bank account. *Carers Allowance* is a benefit you can get if you look after someone.

Why did we start paying individuals to look after their own family members? The whole point of family is that it is an unbreakable bond. *Blood is thicker than water.* We now make interactions between family members financial. *I will only care for you if the State pays me to do it!*

I concede that there will be times when *Carers Allowance* is appropriate and is beneficial to a family and society. Such as if a husband has to give up work to look after his paralysed wife full time. This makes sense to me. But to pay someone to rub cream into their baby is wrong. It is the same as paying children to do chores around the house - it is wrong. They do them for they are part of the family and everyone should contribute where they can to benefit the family.

Did you know we pay people to make poor choices? If you are an alcoholic or drug addict you can claim *Disability Allowance* and receive more money than if you were just simply unemployed. We now reward people to damage themselves. We do not hold individuals to account, we treat them like children and wonder why they cannot cope in life. What next? Rapists claiming back money for condom expenses? Mums demanding more money to parent on a bank holiday?

The more the State gives, the more the State does. We then expect even more to be done. We are tricked into thinking that if we give away our personal responsibility we will get more by doing less. Too good to be true.

The Dark Triad

Negative lifestyles bring out the worst in us. If the majority of society is engaging in, or pursuing such lifestyles, then the trust we have fostered in each other crumbles for we lose societal harmony. If I resent my taxes being spent on 'wasters' and 'cheats,' then I lose my compassion for genuine individuals who need help to get back on their feet. If I live my life as a 'taker,' then every encounter is an opportunity to take something else – I do not see individuals, I see barriers in my way from getting what I want.

If society creates the right environment and we are left to wallow in our misery, then the dark triad of personality traits will manifest – more so in some than others. In psychology, the dark triad comprises of narcissism, Machiavellianism, and psychopathy. They are called 'dark' because of their malevolent qualities.

Research into the dark triad is used in applied psychology, especially within the fields of criminal justice, clinical psychology, and corporate management. The higher your score on these traits, the more likely you are to commit crime, cause social issues and create problems for the people around you. Individuals with higher scores tend to be less compassionate, agreeable, empathetic, satisfied with their lives, and less likely to believe they and others are good. Research has shown that all three traits share characteristics such as a lack of empathy, interpersonal hostility, and interpersonal offensiveness.

Machiavellianism: is characterised by manipulation and exploitation of others, an absence of morality, unemotional callousness, and a higher level of self-interest. Named after the political philosophy promoted by *Niccolò Machiavelli.* People who score high on this trait are cynical (in an amoral self-interest sense), unprincipled, and cold. They believe in manipulation as the way to achieve success. Scores on measures of Machiavellianism correlate negatively with agreeableness and conscientiousness. Machiavellianism is also significantly correlated with psychopathy.

Narcissism: is characterized by grandiosity, pride, egotism, and a lack of empathy. Individuals who score high on narcissism display grandiosity, entitlement, dominance, and superiority. It correlates positively with extraversion and openness. And negatively with agreeableness. Narcissism has also been found to have a significant correlation with psychopathy.

Psychopathy: is characterised by continuous antisocial behaviour, impulsivity, selfishness and remorselessness. The most malevolent of the dark triad. Individuals who score high on psychopathy show low levels of empathy combined with high levels of impulsivity and thrill-seeking.

We have developed social norms and traditions to keep these traits under control for they can destroy a tribe from the inside out. *Thou shall not kill. Thou shall not covet.* Other religions also try to control damaging traits: *And do not mix the truth with falsehood or conceal the truth while you know it* - Shahada (Muslim Declaration of Faith).

California Dreaming

California is failing. It has been for a long while - this is not news in America. The reason seems to be the far-left progressive policies they have enacted over many decades. They have stopped expecting citizens to take responsibility for their own lives – it is now just an option. The state will fix everything for everybody.

When you think of California you imagine beautiful beaches, perfect bodies and glorious sunshine. These are the visions that attract tourists to the *Golden State* from around the world. But this is not the reality for the vast majority of people living in this beautiful part of the US. The Californian dream is over, the nightmare has already begun.

Progressive policies have created a rough sleeping crisis, a mental health epidemic, a crime wave, unaffordable taxes, a lack of homes, and even power blackouts due to green policies. Quality of life is declining and people are beginning to have had enough – an exodus has begun.

Let us look at homelessness – it is at epidemic levels. They have over 150,000 people living on the streets, in vehicles or accessing nightly hostels. This is an incredible number of citizens who have slipped through the safety net - it implies that the safety net is completely incompetent or non-existent.

A large part of this problem is the cost of accommodation. Many people with no drug or mental health issues find themselves with nowhere to live. So they live in their cars. Most have jobs but still cannot find a home they can afford. Green policies have made it extremely difficult to build new homes, so existing ones become increasingly more expensive to buy or rent for the average person.

Research was conducted to investigate if homeless people migrate to the state for the sun and welfare. They found that 92% of individuals were already living in California before becoming homeless - it is a policy problem, not a weather-related problem.

A small section of the homeless is what I call the '*broken people*' – they also live on the streets in the UK but much fewer in number. They are drug addicts with mental health issues, usually caused by childhood trauma. Mental health intervention is needed to repair historic damage and to reduce the need to self-medicate with illegal drugs.

These people are set up to fail in California because of liberal drug policies. The streets in some areas have been handed over to dealers and users. Open drug injection is commonplace, addicts passed out on the pavement and outside shops are the norm.

Venice Beach is a no-go area due to violence which can readily be seen on YouTube. Tents are erected everywhere in the cities – outside shops and homes, in parks and on other available lands. They now have tent cities just like the refugee camps in the Middle East caused by war. Vulnerable individuals have been left to create a living hell for themselves – and we call ourselves compassionate. Change can be achieved, it takes political will and the right policies. Cities such as Houston and Atlanta have halved homelessness in the last decade.

To fund State services requires taxes. Most people are happy to pay their share of tax if it is set at a reasonable rate and local services are competent. There has been a steady exodus out of California for many years, mainly by the rich who can easily move if needed. People say they are fed up with higher taxes alongside a reducing quality of life. When residents and businesses leave they take their taxes with them. The beneficiaries of this exodus have been neighbouring states, such as Texas, Arizona and Nevada. All have lower taxes, cheaper property prices and fewer social issues. To make up for the loss of tax revenue California has to increase taxes for everyone else, this makes more people leave and the death cycle continues.

Margaret Thatcher once said: *"The problem with socialism is that you eventually run out of other people's money."* California is heading in this direction.

This problem is not a new phenomenon. In the 1970s, it was called the *Brain Drain* as people left the UK to avoid a crippling tax rate. In France recently, thousands of millionaires left because of high tax rates. Politicians forget that the rich are mobile, they can move anywhere they wish to in the world. If Brits did it in the 1970s, then imagine how easy it is today. Especially for Californians, for they are only moving to another part of the same country. It is the equivalent of me moving to Scotland. *Easy peasy.*

Why have I suddenly started to care about the plight of Californians? It is a common expectation that US trends make their way over the pond to us. I can think of skateboarding in the 70s, crack cocaine in the 80s, gangster rap in the 90s, and more recently the lunacy of BLM. California should be seen as a preview of where we would be heading if Jeremy Corbyn had been elected in 2019 with his socialist agenda of State dependency. But that does not mean the danger is over – we have only slowed it down.

We are making some of the same mistakes as the *Golden State*. We can see this in the rise in violent crime, rough sleeping and illegal immigration. No one promotes the family unit. Our state education system fails 1 in 5 pupils which is shocking. Government policies constantly promote wokery, progressivism and *'the end is nigh'* green agenda. We need to start to learn from other people's mistakes before we have to learn from our own.

When I close my eyes and dream of California, I see a potential vision of the UK.

California dreaming can be a scary activity these days - best to stay awake, but not 'woke.'

You cannot escape the
responsibility of tomorrow by evading it today.

- Abraham Lincoln

Chapter 7

Personal Responsibility

I have made my career out of promoting personal responsibility as the best life strategy for a successful future. I have done this by pointing out the lack of it in specific individuals and designing projects to help others to accept theirs.

Personal accountability is a character trait that we often admire in others. We like being around people who do not make excuses, take responsibility for their actions, and do not blame others for their mistakes.

When you have a sense of personal responsibility, it means you are willing to accept and live by your own choices, decisions and actions. You do not seek to blame others for convenience but reflect on how you could have acted differently to achieve a better outcome.

Life is a series of choices. The consequences of these choices have far-reaching effects on you and the people around you. Understanding that you have a direct impact on the quality of your life is what personal responsibility is all about. You create both positive and negative outcomes.

I watched an interview with the American actor *Terry Crews*. You may know him from the *Expendables* film series – he is a muscular black man with a bald head. I first came across him in the film *White Chicks*. During this interview, he discussed his acting break by getting a small speaking part in the first *Expendables* film with Sylvester Stallone. But he was not happy with his part, he was not happy with the way he was being treated on set. He was just not happy. At the end of a particular day's filming, he went back to his hotel to think about his situation. He suddenly realised he was being stupid and ungrateful. He had a part in a major action film with many well-established action heroes. He decided to change his attitude and embrace his opportunity. He arrived on set early the next day with a new outlook and lots of energy. He would make the most of this gift laid out before him. He took all constructive criticism positively and tried to do what was being asked of him. He gave 100% every day. He offered to do more, he helped on set where he could, and supported anyone who needed a hand. Over the months of filming, his part started to grow. He got more scenes. He got more lines. He ended up with a fantastic solo scene which is one of the classic moments in the whole film. The more he took responsibility and worked hard within the team, the more he was rewarded. It is common sense that others want to work with such people. Why would they not? Such people make everyone else's life easier and less stressful.

Let us look at what it takes to stop making excuses, blaming others and accept our responsibility.

1. Communication Skills

You have to be able to communicate, this means listening and also expressing what you want. Vagueness leads to a lack of action and the wrong outcomes. Asking questions enables you to fully understand what is needed, what is expected, and what is desired.

Hardly anything goes to plan. We need to ask for feedback to ensure we are on the right track, as well as to self reflect so we can improve and learn from our mistakes.

Assumption is the mother of all mistakes.
- Eugene Lewis Fordsworthe

2. Know Your Limit

There is no point in taking on so much responsibility that you crumble under the weight. For you then become a burden on others which negates the reason why you were taking on responsibility in the first place. You are only one person and cannot take on responsibility for the world.

Taking on more is beneficial but it must be done sensibly. You must ensure what you are responsible for is under control and producing the outcomes desired. When at this point, you can think about taking on a little bit more and then a little bit more. Test the water first. Do not plunge into the deep end and then figure out if you can swim. It is not a failure to know your limit and pass up on the opportunity to take on more.

Nothing limits you like not knowing your limitations.
- Tom Hayes

3. Humility

You are not a God, you are just a human with many flaws, inadequacies and a huge lack of knowledge. You need to be honest with yourself and with other people about what you are capable of doing and not doing. Pride may distort your reasoning, especially if you want to be everything to everyone. Asking for help from others is not negating your personal responsibility. It is accepting that we all need help to succeed – failure we can easily do on our own.

Humility has the toughest hide. **- Friedrich Nietzsche**

4. Self Control

The person who causes you the most problem is you. We seek easy solutions where none exist, we use sticking plasters on problems so we can move on to another. We are tempted by quick fixes which do not work. We rush decisions without thinking them through. We have to control our impulses and use logic, otherwise poor decisions are made which lead to unwanted outcomes. Only you can control you.

Every act of self-control leads to a sense of self-respect.
- Abraham Low

5. Courage

It takes courage to put your head above the parapet and do what needs to be done, for people may point and laugh if you fail. By taking on responsibility you also take on the possibility of failure – and you will own that failure. But this is the wrong way to look at it. What if you are successful? To build courage, you need to face what you are afraid of and overcome it. Fear is a product of the unknown, and if you can accept the unknown, fear will have less of an impact on you.

Courage comes with action. **- Gail Blanke**

6. Persistence

Regardless of what life throws at you, you have to keep moving forward and doing what needs to be done. Giving up is not an option – take it off the table forever. You cannot go from 1 to 100 in one jump. You have to do the 98 steps in between. It may be laborious but persistence will get you to the end, eventually. If you fail or make a mistake then learn from it and try again. You may fail a second time and learn something that was not obvious the first time around. Then you continue to try again.

Failure cannot cope with persistence. **- Napoleon Hill**

7. Be Authentic

You do what needs to be done because that is what you expect of yourself. It does not matter what others say, especially people who do not have your best interests at heart.

You may ask for and need help, we all do. Do not try to be an inferior version of someone you wish to be. Do things your way. Being authentic means being honest with yourself and others about who you are, what you mean, and what you want. It is better to be genuine at all times for this fosters trust and respect in others.

To be authentic is to be at peace with your imperfections.
- Simon Sinek

8. Be Organised

You have to keep track of your personal and professional responsibilities. This is so you know where you are up to, what needs doing next, when things need doing by, and what to prioritise. Otherwise, it all falls like a house of cards. This may mean using tools, such as weekly planners, to-do lists, calendars, or anything else that may help. Avoid putting things off until the last minute as unforeseen circumstances can scupper your plans. Do not fall into the trap of prioritising the tasks you enjoy doing, for when you look at your list later, only difficult and unenjoyable tasks remain.

For every minute spent organising, an hour is earned.
– Anonymous.

I describe personal responsibility as the acknowledgement that you are the captain of your own ship and the creator of your own destiny. This does not mean you can guarantee calm seas. We have no control over external factors such as storms, hurricanes, and volcanic eruptions. We have to mitigate against such perils, learn from them if possible, but carry on with the journey despite the inconvenience and danger. Throwing your hands up in the air and blaming others in the middle of a crisis only guarantees failure. In its most simplistic form, accepting personal responsibility means you are no longer a child - only children do not have the responsibility to take care of themselves.

If life is a game then we only get one go at it. It is not like an old fashioned video game where we get three lives and can be careless until our last one. Modern-day versions are more generous and give you unlimited lives. In real life, you only get one go, we have to make the most of it while being sensible.

This leads us to the question of who do you think is in the best position to make top-quality decisions concerning your life, dreams and wishes? Not just for today, but for decisions that will affect you in the medium and long term. Who is the person that will benefit the most from your success? Who will have to pay the consequences of poor choices?

The answer to all these questions is YOU.

Why would you want someone to be the captain of your ship? To make the choices, to dictate the direction of sail, to plot the course. It is your ship that will be destroyed or pillaged, not theirs! A hired captain is insulated from the negative decisions they make, for the losses are all yours as the owner, not theirs as an employee.

There are benefits of allowing others to run your life for you and make your decisions. It makes your life seem easier in the short term. No worrying about things for someone else will do it for you. Less anxiety about the future for it is not in your hands. It all sounds great. But just like *King Midas* and his desire for gold, what you think is beneficial in the short term does not always deliver what is beneficial in the medium and long term. Everything he touched turned to gold. Such a wonderful gift. But he could not eat, touch or love – what he touched he destroyed. He was living in a hell of his own construction. What we want is not always what is good for us.

The Myth: King Midas found the wandering Silenus, the satyr and companion of the god Dionysus. For his kind treatment of Silenus he was rewarded by Dionysus with a wish. The king wished that all he touched would turn to gold, but when his food became gold he nearly starved to death as a result, he then realized his error. Dionysus then granted his release by having him bathe in a river.

Some people seem to look for excuses so they can dismiss their responsibility with their heads held high. Religions are good at this, if you only have faith then everything will work out in the end. The Greek Gods played with humans like action figures. They moved the pieces, created problems and rewarded individuals – people were pawns in a cosmic Action Man game. Modern religions still have a flavour of this thinking – *God moves in mysterious ways!*

When I was growing up, horoscopes were a big deal. They were in every newspaper and on daytime TV shows. It was a common request from strangers to ask to quickly look at your newspaper to check out their horoscope for the day. Imagine people asking you in public to read out their daily dose of made-up *mumbo jumbo*. But people did. Why? They did not want to believe that their life was totally their responsibility and in their hands. They wanted to believe that magical forces were at play, for that meant that the problems they have may not be their fault. A comfort blanket for weak individuals. Similar logic manifests when you have a gambling problem. You think one big win will solve all your problems – you just need one piece of luck. The reality is that when you do win big, you just gamble it all away for you have an addiction and no self-control. The spinning roulette wheel or an unturned playing card holds your fate. Losing is not your fault for bad luck was around that day, you were powerless.

After a lifetime of accepting no responsibility, it can come as a huge shock when you start down this path. Negative outcomes happen all the time, not necessarily your fault, it is just a fact of life. When this happens it can knock you right back to square one and you give up trying for what is the point? The realisation that there will always be external factors messing with your life is a truism that many cannot cope with, so decide to hand everything over to chance.

This is where the phrase '*try, and try again*' comes into play. I passed my driving test on the third attempt. I passed my English O-level (GCSE equivalent) on my 6th exam. It took me thirteen years to stop stuttering. We all have problems and setbacks, they are never an excuse to give up. Perseverance is the key.

Begging To Ignore Responsibility

Adrian had his brand new trainers stolen. He was a recovering homeless drug addict living in a halfway house until his support worker deemed him ready to live in his own place. We got him a part-time job cleaning in a building site canteen, he did well. We put him through a week's training course so he was qualified to work on a building site and arranged for his H&S card (CSCS card) – a legal requirement. We had a full-time job lined up for him once he got his card. He enjoyed his new job and the increase in money.

One day he came into my office to say he was quitting. He was furious. I tried to calm him and sat him down. He had just finished his shift and went to the changing rooms to change out of his work clothes before he headed home. His brand new trainers were missing. They were only 2 days old and cost £150. I asked him if someone had broken into his locker? They had not. He had not put them in his locker. I asked why. He did not have a reason. That was the whole point of every worker having a free lockable locker, even the padlocks were provided for free.

He had made a mistake. He knew it, that was why he was so angry. He was upset with himself for being so stupid and leaving something valuable on display. It was a weekly occurrence that someone had their lunch stolen, never mind a pair of £150 new shoes. The site had thieves, we all knew this.

This theft was absolutely not his fault. He had done nothing wrong. The only person to blame for the incident was the theft who took the shoes. But common sense tells you that in society we have individuals who will steal anything you have not bolted down. It is not fair or right, but it is true. Adrian knew this deep down inside.

Rather than take away a valuable lesson from this loss to ensure it never happened again, he needed someone to blame and punish. His nominated 'persecutor' was his employer. He would punish 'them' by removing his labour. *They would surely suffer now and feel his pain.*

He resigned there and then. I could not talk him out of it. He had been wronged, someone needed to be punished. He told me he deserved respect and to be treated better. It was like talking to a child who has no idea of how the world really works.

Surprisingly, he phoned me a month later to apologise and admit he was wrong in the way he handled the situation. He asked for another chance for employment. We have a policy of *'no last chance'* meaning we will continue to work with anyone regardless of how many times they mess up. It only takes one opportunity to stick and a life changes forever. He came back purely for the money, he was still sour, after 2 months he left again. An opportunity for him to improve his life forever was wasted because of the theft of a pair of trainers. Imagine that. You give up a better life because some scum-bag steals your shoes. The human mind is complicated and easily twisted to placate the ego.

My charity had a small office within a construction firm in Spinningfields in Manchester city centre for a year. They were building a new tower block called *20 Stories* and the adjoining *Ivy* restaurant next door. They graciously offered us free offices – the whole team were amazing and raised money for us.

One morning their office manager came to see me under the stairs, for we had a Harry Potter office. She explained that she saw the same homeless man every morning on the footbridge that connected Spinningfields in Manchester, to New Bailey in Salford. This morning she stopped and chatted to him. She knew we worked with the homeless so came to see me and enquire what could be done.

Our outreach manager did not know this man so he went to the bridge the next day to find him. The man was rough sleeping, as opposed to most beggars who are not. He had a tent and small encampment set up under the bridge. We spent time trying to get to know him and see what help he wanted. He did not want any help or support from us. We hear this all the time, but over time defences come down and we discover what they want or are willing to accept. This did not happen in this case.

He had a good beggar's narrative. He did not want help for he was not in distress or in need. He had picked life on the streets and enjoyed it. He paid no bills. He answered to no one. He had no stress. He was free. He rejected all personal responsibility to live the life he was meant to live before the modern world ruined it for everyone. He was convincing. It was obvious he believed what he was saying while saying it.

We kept visiting him over a few weeks to chip away at his narrative and continued to offer him help and support. The office manager also continued to speak with him daily on her way to work and updated us with her conversations when relevant. One day he just disappeared and we never saw him again.

He was the only person we ever met that explained his rejection of his responsibility was to gain liberation, freedom and contentment. He achieved what he set out to achieve – but at what price? He lived in squalor under a bridge like a troll, relied on handouts and begged to survive. His physical health was obviously deteriorating. He was paying the price everyone pays for such poor choices - he paid the *King Midas* price. What he desired was killing him.

Taking on responsibility is difficult, if it was easy then we would not have a problem with people rejecting it. We are born with no responsibility and expect others to do everything for us because we are children. But as we get older, our parents need to place appropriate responsibilities onto our shoulders so we become used to bearing a load. This can be as simple as cleaning our bedroom, putting our toys away and washing the dinner plates. I am not a believer in paying children to do chores for this does not foster personal responsibility. But an expectation that life should compensate you for doing what is your responsibility to do. The lesson a child needs to learn is that everyone in the family contributes to the well-being of the family. They are a team.

Sometimes it is easier to pay someone to do what needs to be done, but over time an expectation is developed which becomes the norm. We know that in life there are many things you have to do for 'free' if you want to improve, better yourself or succeed. If we are raised to only engage in immediately beneficial opportunities then we miss out on medium and long term opportunities. These usually offer a greater reward down the road. Instant gratification is not a long term successful life strategy.

The first time my charity worked in Blackley in North Manchester we targeted a local park. We wanted to engage local kids and start some project work around crime, personal safety and positive choices. The kids were great but did not want to engage in any project work, they were happy to just chat and have conversations. But they did not want to enrol on a project that would take some commitment on their part.

My manager asked me if we could arrange a trip for the kids as an incentive if they completed our project. Alton Towers, Blackpool and go-carting were put forward as possible excursions. This did not sit comfortably with me so I asked where this idea had come from. My manager told me this was what the kids had suggested if we wanted them involved in our project. I was shocked. It needed some thought.

I realised that their expectation of 'youth workers' was a *quid pro quo* relationship. We do what you want us to do, and then you take us somewhere we want to go. *A favour for a favour. Tit for tat. You scratch my back, and I'll scratch yours. One hand washes the other.* This goes to the very heart of the problem of poor youth work delivered by unskilled youth workers – the need for bribery.

If you have to pay someone to accept your help then they are not looking to better themselves or learn new skills, they are turning up for all the wrong reasons. This is not a good strategy when trying to build trust or change behaviour. But in this example, years of being offered something for nothing created a beggar's mentality in the young people. You can say that the council youth workers did more harm than good in the real world. But in the council world, they ticked all the boxes their bosses required so they could produce reports that no one would read.

Needless to say, we offered them nothing to the dismay of my staff. I had to remind everyone that a good youth worker does not need gimmicks to facilitate their job, they use their skill as a professional. I had never told them that their job was going to be easy working in my charity, for it is not – I am demanding. But the reward they can secure is the ability to change lives for the better. Within a few months, we had the kids fully engaged – it just took time to change their expectations and for them to understand the benefit of working with us. Lazy staff have to buy engagement. I will have none of it in my charity.

A similar issue I have come across many times is false accounting. Not businesses 'cooking the books' to avoid paying tax, but individuals on welfare benefits thinking about if they should get a paid job or not. It usually goes along the lines of.....

> *I get £400 on Universal Credit. £650 housing benefit. £150 council tax relief – all monthly. That's a total of £1200. I can get a job at £8.50 per hour, 40 hours a week. That's £1473 per month or £334 a week. After paying tax, I would get £302 per week. I currently get £277 a week on benefits. Why would I work 40 hours a week for £25? That's £0.63 an hour!*

These figures are made-up for mathematical ease, but you get my point. This person is not looking at how much they earn, just at what the additional income will be once welfare benefits are removed. This type of mentality traps people on benefits because who in their right mind would want to work for £0.63 per hour? But this way of thinking is all wrong, they actually earn £8.50 per hour. If we can rebrand many welfare benefits as 'State Charity' and stop referring to them as an entitlement, then this may reduce dependency over time. We need to pull back the pink and fluffy cover that hides what they are - handouts. It is charity, paid for by other people because you cannot take care of yourself. Let us start being truthful.

I have dealt with many such conversations by highlighting all the non-financial benefits of accepting a job. Making new friends, improved social life, better mental health, no more begging off the State, ability to hold your head up high and pay your own way. Pride. Confidence. Self-respect. Plus, the opportunities that will arise to increase your rate of pay if you work hard and put in the effort.

What some people on benefits actually want is *Universal Basic Income* (UBI), even though they have probably never heard of it. It does not exist anywhere in the real world. UBI is a State payment given to all citizens of a country, it is not means-tested or dependent upon seeking work. It is set at a rate that allows people to pay for all their basic needs, including rent, utilities and food. If you decide to work then you still keep your UBI payment. Sounds amazing. It is the latest of a long line of silly socialist ideas that would never work in reality. It would bankrupt the country and contribute to the trend of turning the masses into beggars dependent upon the State – exactly what a good socialist wants for this is how you control the people.

Several years ago, I was watching a documentary on TV about welfare dependency. A particular scene always stayed with me for it showed the mental gymnastics people play to validate their demand for more. A particular part of the documentary involved a group of teenage mums discussing life on benefits and the difficulties incurred. One young lady explained why she felt payments to her should be increased. Her deceased uncle had worked all his life and paid taxes. He died single with no children. He had paid into the system all his life and never took anything out of it. Therefore, she thought she was entitled to a little bit extra because her family member contributed and he would have wanted her to have it.

She was not content or grateful that the State was taking care of her and her baby because she was not financially capable of doing so herself. It was her birthright to waste a decade of state-funded education, never expect to work, get pregnant to an invisible man, and beg off the taxpayer. Unbelievable entitlement.

This TV programme reminded me of when I worked at the reception desk in a council office for a few weeks in East Manchester. I dealt with many members of the local community concerning many issues. After a few days, I found a common theme from residents when they were asking for something extra or for free. They would look me in the eyes and proudly inform me that they were a single mum. They would then wait for me to speak. I am sure they expected me to fill up, take them by the hand and express my adoration at their bravery. I never did.

The fact that they would state their parental status meant they thought or had learnt, that such an announcement would be beneficial. Looking back, it was definitely a version of victimhood mentality. The 'single parent' label had become a badge of honour and a victim status symbol, not a sign of someone who made poor choices. No one would dare ask these mothers why they did not keep their legs closed, use freely available birth control, or pick a decent man to breed with. *This was sacrilege. Heresy. Gross misconduct.* I kept my mouth shut, I was a lot smarter then.

A question no one discusses is how did we get ourselves into such a mess? Why are we raising individuals with no aspiration, pride, or self-respect? Where did this sense of entitlement come from?

Begging For Purpose

Mike was a beggar. He did not sleep on the streets for he was too intelligent to fall that low but he was homeless. He was the self-proclaimed *King of the Squats* and ran many over time in Manchester city centre. He was approx mid-30s but very hard to tell when you do not look after yourself. He had researched and read up on the relevant legislation regarding squatting. He knew his rights and exactly what the law stated. He reclaimed empty commercial buildings in the city centre (which means he broke into them), changed the locks, and placed signs advertising that the building was now residential habitation. He knew exactly what he was doing, he knew how long it would take to be removed legally. By which time, he would have a new potential squat reconnoitred and ready to go. He was an intelligent man, not just for a homeless person, but for any person.

Mike was a warrior, he was a social justice warrior. But not one of the new breed of woke social justice warriors. He was a 1980s, stood on a picket line, bare-knuckle fighting with the police, kind of social justice warrior. He could be violent and was proud of it. He was small in stature, probably bullied when younger, learnt how to fight and developed a Napoleon complex. We have all met someone similar. I remember a police Chief Superintendent who was the classic Napoleon complex sufferer, he now runs the anti-terrorist department.

The first time we came across Mike he was sitting outside a city centre supermarket with a paper cup at his feet and his head buried in a book. He was constantly reading. He was a prolific reader. He would discuss politics, culture, and any of his many ideas, he had an opinion on everything. After a discussion on politics, a staff member bought him a second-hand copy of the book *The Prince* by Machiavelli. Mike could quote parts of the book in conversation but had never read it whole.

Just because he was very intelligent did not mean he was not severely damaged by life. He was. I do not recall his exact personal story or if he ever shared it with us. He probably did not for I cannot remember him ever talking about himself, only ever what he was going to do for other people. He never looked backwards, only to the next fight and why it was righteous. Many people do not want to open their memory box for that is where the monsters live. It may have taken a long time to get them in the box, best not to let them out.

Initially, he spun many of my staff his beggar's narrative and they all fell for it. He was a talented beggar. He told us he made £100 cash per afternoon. He had a sob story about living on the streets, helping other rough sleepers to his detriment, and being a voice for the unheard. We had limited resources as a small charity so only spent time with people who actively wanted to move on to a better life. Mike did not. It may sound awful but he was wasting our time and stopping us from helping other people in need.

Things changed when we employed a new manager to run the outreach project. He had a lifetime of experience working with disenfranchised, hard to reach, and broken people. He had heard it all before and was no fool. He was introduced to Mike during a shift and they had a chat. A relationship developed. Mike did not ask for help and my manager did not offer any. Mutual respect was fostered. Mike started to update my manager on who was new to the streets and where they were sleeping or begging. We found this information very helpful and it allowed us to offer vulnerable individuals the support they needed to get off the streets a lot sooner. He also started to advertise to the rough sleeping community who we were and what we could offer.

After a short while, Mike started to invite us into his squat so we could offer residents help and support to move on and access accommodation. The majority of residents had no intention of moving on and found the lifestyle comfortable. But some were only staying there because it was better than sleeping on the cold hard street. They took the least worse option available to them but wanted something better and permanent.

Mike had a girlfriend and she was pregnant. She looked like the typical runaway, maybe late teens but difficult to be sure. We convinced him he needed a better life for his woman and child. He agreed. We came up with a plan with him. He would volunteer for the project as an outreach worker to enable him to feel he had not abandoned the vulnerable. We would source him a proper job that paid a wage. And we would find him his own accommodation and sort out the deposit and first month's rent. We did not get into the details but he said he was not moving in with his girlfriend. A homeless pregnant woman in the UK has no accommodation issues, in fact, if you do not accept accommodation then you will probably lose your baby to social services.

We placed him on several in-house training sessions to upskill him to become a volunteer. He started working a couple of shifts a week. We found him a part-time job with one of our commercial partners cleaning up on a building site and taking deliveries. It was a perfect position for him for we were also based with this company and we could support him on a daily basis. Lastly, we started to speak to landlords about shared accommodation for this is the only option available to a single man.

We invited him to one of our bi-annual charity team 'get togethers' – an opportunity for staff, trustees, ambassadors and volunteers to get together, hear about the charity's progress and have a few drinks afterwards. Mike gave a small talk about what it is like to be rough sleeping. People cried. Many people told me afterwards that the session was the best one they had ever attended. We started to invite more service users we had helped to future events.

Our plan for him worked well, to begin with. He hit the ground running. The bosses at his job were impressed and wanted him full time. His volunteering was fruitful - he got results where we never dreamed we could have succeeded. After six weeks, we found a landlord that had a room available and willing to accept Mike with no references. It was all looking good.

At about three weeks into the plan, we started to see cracks. Mike had phoned in sick - these things happen. The company thought they would help him out by paying him for his sick days to which he was not entitled. Mike noticed this. More sick days followed. More payments followed. We were told, but could never prove, on at least one of the days he phoned in sick he spent the day begging. We asked for Mike not to be paid if he did not work his shift.

It all came to a head when we took him to view the shared accommodation we had found for him. We drove him to the house, a standard 3-bed semi-detached. The bedrooms were hired out to individuals who then share the bathroom, kitchen and living room. The same sort of arrangement as some student accommodation. We met the landlady there and were shown around.

Mike was not impressed. After a few minutes, he said he was not interested in the accommodation, it was not up to his standard and he deserved a lot better. He actually used the word 'deserved.' The landlady was not happy with us for wasting her time. He did not say a word on the journey back to the city centre. The next day he phoned to say he was resigning from his paid job and as a volunteer for the charity. He said the main reason was that being paid £8.50 ph was disgraceful. He never spoke to us again.

A few days after his resignation, people started to mention that they had borrowed him money for different reasons. He had needed electricity, he needed food, his pregnant girlfriend needed something, or he had no money for lunch. There were many reasons given, all lies, all a beggar's narrative. It became clear what we had done. We had let a beggar into a workspace where he picked off people one by one with sob stories. They had no immunity to a talented beggar. Mike had a field day. He was like a lion who accidentally finds himself in a secure enclosure full of goats. It was easy pickings – *shooting fish in a barrel.*

The member of staff who arranged everything for him was devastated. Six months of work down the tube. This staff member never recovered from this failure, lost all passion for the job and eventual we had to let him go. It was sad to see. He had personally invested himself in Mike. Gone above and beyond. And probably felt embarrassed that he had been sucked into a beggar's narrative like many other people before. It is difficult to help someone who only tells you what they think you want to hear.

Mike was intelligent enough to know he wanted better in life and what he would have to do to achieve it. But he was broken, damaged and afraid. He had learnt how to take the easy path in life by running away, blaming others, and convincing himself that he was a victim. When threatened with reality and offered choices, he would retreat to his safe space of victimhood. He would seek to be the hero again in his own story.

He would become a street version of Luke Skywalker, Sarah Connor, Captain America, or Gandhi. Even a Mancunian version of George Floyd – *the man who gave his life so others could riot and loot.*

Begging To Be Right

Personal responsibility is my religion. I am a born again *personal 'responsibilitier.'* I saw the light. My guardian angel looked upon me during an evening of larger and garlic bread. He nudged me onto the path of righteousness with an overheard conversation. It happened at my friend's house-warming party, this miracle took place in front of all my friends – no one noticed, yet it changed my life. *Praise The Lord.*

My friend's wife was chatting to another friend about a recruitment drive at her workplace at Manchester airport. They needed 40 new airport ground staff for two new flights to America. My friend was constantly complaining about his job, but never doing anything about it. He asked if an application form could be secured? The answer was YES.

It was at this point that I chipped in. I had just folded my small business and was unemployed. When I say business, I mean my sideline of buying and selling – I had one good year in a decade of trading. I needed some income and was trying to figure out what to do next to become a millionaire. A few months working at the airport sounded good. Some money and access to cheap flights was a great package.

I applied. I was successful. It gave me my first proper job. I had structure, a regular wage, and work friends. I soon realised that an average regular income was more beneficial than an irregular one. I started to plan out my future for I knew what I had coming in. This one concept changed my life. If I had a plan, then I was responsible for that plan. I needed to implement it otherwise what was the point of creating the plan. I had personal responsibility. And like all personal responsibility, I had assigned it to myself – for no one else can delegate such a task.

Whatever happened to my friend who asked for a job application at the same time? He got an application but failed to fill in and send it off. He had a reason at the time that I do not remember. The truth was he felt more comfortable complaining about what he knew than taking a chance on trying something else and realising he was still unhappy. Learnt helplessness.

I was 32 years old when I got the airport job. Had I accepted some of my personal responsibility before this? Yes, I had. But I was not a true believer – see Chapter Two for my sins.

I was like an average Christian in the UK today – I say I am a Christian so therefore I must be one. They go to Church for weddings and Christenings, pray to God when they want something, and watch the *10 Commandments* film every couple of years. But they do not live by the commandments or follow the teachings of Christ. Fair weathered religious folk.

I took responsibility for my everyday life. I washed my face, brushed my teeth, and fed myself. I had many different types of relationships to maintain: family, friends, and romantic. I did not lie (too much), I did not cheat (except sometimes claiming benefits). I was looking after the essentials in my life but rejecting the overarching responsibility of long term planning. My mistake was I was waiting for a lucky break. I did not know that luck was earned, I just thought it came around and I was waiting for my turn.

In one way, I was lucky. My life could have been so different if one of my silly choices had gone the wrong way. Sometimes you cannot reject your personal responsibility after the fact, regardless of how much you wish you could. A friend of mine has a brother who when 17 years old chipped in with friends to buy a motorbike to mess around on in a local park. When it was his turn the brakes seized and he ploughed into a tree and was paralysed. I worked in a pub when two friends decided to go outside to settle an argument with their fists. The first punch landed, and a man fell smashing the back of his head on the corner of the pavement. Dead instantly.

What would have become of me if I had broken my back when I jumped off a three-story hotel roof into a swimming pool in Spain? Drunk and in my twenties. I went through the water like a hot knife through butter and smashed my back on the bottom of the pool. I climbed out to the smile of many a girl, but my back was sore.

A friend who was in the army asked me to hire a car in Manchester and drive to Gatwick airport to pick him up – he would pick up the expenses. Not a problem. I was not working that day so I and another friend thought it would be a fun day out. Up to that point in my life, I had never owned a car, I had only ever had vans for I worked as a market trader. A smooth driving new car felt amazing. So quiet, so responsive, so comfortable. I headed to the M6 South. I took a longer way to get to the motorway so I could test out the car on smaller roads. Mistake. I was on an A road approaching a bend when I checked my speed. I was doing over 60 miles per hour. Shit. I started to slow down as fast as I could while keeping in control of the vehicle. 55 miles per hour. 50 miles per hour. 45 miles per hour. The bend was upon us. What to do was the decision I had to make in a split decision. I could not make the bend at my speed, or at least I did not think I could. The area surrounding the road was all grassed and led to fields. I held the steering wheel straight as I continued to brake. I shot across to the other side of the road, hit the curb, went air-born, spun around and came to a standstill facing the road. As we both looked at each other, we were jolted out of our shock by the sound of an 18 wheel juggernaut as it drove past us. If we have been 2 seconds later we would have crashed right into this truck head-on. *Dead meat.* Believe it or not, there was not a mark on the car. The only damage was mechanical. Probably caused by hitting the curb, for when we drove over 50 miles per hour the car started to shake.

Begging For Heroes

The *Marvel* film franchise has dominated the cinema for 15 years. Has anyone wondered why? What is it about these films that we love? And at the same time, why have more young men opted out of society by rejecting their personal responsibility? We have seen the development of communities such as *Men Going Their Own Way* (MGTOW), and *Involuntary Celibates* (Incels). In a popular culture full of superheroes, why are people not copying what they see on the big screen?

I am not a big fan of these superhero films. Too simplistic. Too much CGI. I remember watching the first *Captain America* film when released on video, for parts were filmed in Manchester city centre. 1940s Manhattan was created in the city's Northern Quarter. Years later, I tried to watch *Black Panther* and one of the *Avengers* films but turned them off after twenty minutes. Bored.

Recently, I could not find anything to watch on TV so decided to rewatch *Captain America*. I enjoyed it more than I remembered, so the next evening I watched the first *Avengers* film. It was while watching the differences between the characters that I realised what unites them as a team: personal responsibility.

The Captain America character is the child within us all. He sees everything as black and white, good vs evil, right or wrong. He picks the correct path regardless of the personal consequences. He is a protector. He was bullied as a child - he now has the power to stop bullies so feels a sense of duty. He is the simplified version of who we all wish we were. A decent, honourable person who protects the weaker in society.

Iron Man is a different character altogether. He is a grown-up version of Captain America. He understands that life is not black or white – he understands nuance. He has many character flaws and is aware of them. He is narcissistic, selfish, spoilt and untrusting. He sees the dangers in the world and also in the hearts of men. He is a cynic, yet, spends his time and money improving the world for mankind. A rich white boy trying to improve the lives of the less fortunate – a type of social justice warrior? Sometimes we like him, sometimes we do not.

The Hulk is what lies within us all - destruction and rage. It is always brimming below the surface and in need of constant attention to keep it under control. Dr Banner, aka Hulk, is a very intelligent man, yet he cannot always control his rage. The message is clear, this type of fury is not just the purview of the stupid, uneducated or common man, but within us all. I saw this in the 1980s when arrested football hooligans turned out to be solicitors, bankers and school teachers.

The conflict between Thor and Loki is the classic battle of the

Gods. Good versus evil. Thor is a kick-arse version of Jesus – sent to earth to save mankind. Loki is the Devil - using tricks and deception to gain the power to rule over the world. Brothers in conflict. They represent the two sides of us, the constant internal battle of light over dark. Loki is the resentment that resides within. Always looking to blame someone for the trials and tribulations of life, never accepting personal responsibility. Victimhood mentality.

We had heroes before *Marvel*, every generation and culture has them. In my lifetime, I have wanted to be John Wayne, Clint Eastwood, Stallone and Schwarzenegger. The highest-earning actor over the last few years has been The Rock – aka Dwayne Johnson. He kicks the arse of the bad guys, never abuses his power and protects the vulnerable. A classic hero.

We prefer characters who are not immortal for this is where we see bravery. Captain America can be hurt and injured, yet he stands back up and moves forward toward the enemy. Iron Man pushes a nuclear missile into a wormhole to save others with no expectation of surviving. Luckily, he falls back to earth and is saved by another Avenger. It is the perseverance we admire, the self-sacrifice, the ability to stand back up after being knocked down. Courage.

It ain't how hard you hit; it's about how hard you can get hit, and keep moving forward. - **Rocky Balboa**

There is a message in the *Marvel* universe for us all, especially for young men struggling to find their path in life. It is around taking on responsibility, looking out for others, and being true to yourself. This all sounds a bit wishy-washy, so let me explain a little better.

The first message is to be aware of the monster that resides within - your own Hulk. This is the part of you that seeks destruction, whether this is name-calling, spreading rumours, bullying, violence or much worse. Read a history book to see the outcome of man's rage. We must control our anger for it leads to a dark place, not only for us but for society. Dr Banner spends his life running away from his anger and is tortured at the hands of loneliness. Be the master of your beast, not its victim.

Life is complicated. Problems are rarely as simple as right or wrong. We need to operate at a higher level so we make more productive choices – this requires education. We need to be more like the brilliant inventor Tony Stark, aka Iron Man, so we can see the detail of the problem. Knowledge is power.

When in doubt, do what you feel is right. We all have an inbuilt moral compass and need to trust it. Captain America's instinct is to always take the course of action that he feels is moral. He does not think about it, he acts. When in doubt, and let's be honest - we are always in doubt of what to do, we should do what we feel is moral. As opposed to doing nothing - not acting when you should is cowardice. No one wants to be a coward. We make excuses to try to fool ourselves when we know we have chosen unwisely.

These films are modern myths and legends. They are successful for we see ourselves in the characters, or at least, see who we wish we were. We cannot be Captain America, but maybe we can take on part of his essence – and do what is right. We do not have the brilliance of Tony Stark, but we can educate ourselves a little more to improve our lives and society. We will never turn into a green Hulk, but we are all capable of evil so be careful of our choices. We need to be aware of Loki and watch out for the lies that will tempt us, for they do not lead to fulfilment.

We need more superheroes – for they embrace their responsibility. We need young people to want to be them, idolise them, and act out their characteristics. Their first mission should be to accept responsibility for their own words and actions. Own what you say and be judged on your actions.

Act like the person you want to be and you will be one step closer to becoming it. When in doubt, remember the words of a captain who wore blue tights.

> *For as long as I can remember, I just wanted to do what was right.* - **Captain America**

I remember an incident where I rescued a damsel in distress, her imagination was a terrifying monster and was stalking her. I called around to see a friend for a chat. His girlfriend Janet was not well and was lying on the settee. She explained that she had been out the night before with some friends and had her drink spiked. I started to ask some questions for I had always been suspicious of such claims.

She had gone out straight from work and did not have anything to eat. I asked for a rundown of where they had been and who bought a drink in each bar. We worked out she had had seven double vodka and cokes - the figure was more than she originally remembered.

Why did she think she had been spiked? She told me she suddenly felt ill and threw up outside the pub. I asked her a simple question. If some evil man wanted to drug and rape you, why would he administer a drug that made you throw up all over yourself? Or would he prefer to make you more docile with much less vomit? And finally, how did he think he was ever going to get you away from your friends?

After the conversation she thanked me. She felt much better for she now realised that she had not been spiked and had not been in danger. She had just drunk too much on an empty stomach and then scared herself silly with an urban legend perpetuated by other women.

She took onboard her personal responsibility for her safety and well-being. She had learnt a valuable lesson about alcohol and its effects. She knew she had made poor choices that evening. But now she knew she had made them, she knew that next time she would make better ones. Thinking that a stranger had power over her scared her silly, and rightly so. But the rest of her day lying on the settee being waited upon by my friend ended as I left. She was not a victim, she was not special. She was a very naughty girl who drank too much and cried foul when she received an outcome she did not want.

Begging For No Accountability

Another time, I called around to the home of a different friend to borrow a power tool. He was in a terrible mood. He did not like to lend out his tools for he was a tradesman and was tired of his tools going missing when he needed them. Understandable.

I asked him what was wrong, he vented his fury in the form of an incident at work. His boss had accused him of lying and phoning in sick on false pretences – my friend was not happy about it. It was an affront to his dignity, a slight against his self-respect, a damaging assertion that would reflect upon his reputation.

He had not gone to work that day because his son had been rushed to hospital with an asthma attack. My friend had gone with him and stayed at the hospital – he had been worried sick. Understandable.

I asked how his son was doing? The answer shocked me. The son was doing fine because he did not have asthma, had not had an asthma attack and did not visit any hospital. I pointed out to my friend that he was actually lying to his boss, so why was he so upset about being called out.

He then explained that I had missed the whole point of his story. He had been lying but his boss could not prove it – so how dare he say it was so. His logic was that his boss was either an inconsiderate man who did not care about sick children, or thought that he was the type of man that would lie and be dishonest. I again informed him that he was a liar and his boss was right. I was told again that I did not get the point being made. His boss had no proof he was lying, so could not be in a position to make such a claim. It was insulting. Innocent until proven guilty.

I asked why did he need a day off work? He had been offered a day's work on another project that was in trouble and paying silly money. Three-quarters of a day's work in an emergency situation with only 12 hours of notice paid a week's wage. He could not turn it down. He had phoned in sick several times before, as well as taken some annual leave, to complete such work. But he had never been accused of lying before.

I tried for another hour to make him see the flaw in his thinking but he could not comprehend the paradox. The reality of the situation did not matter for it could not be proved he was a liar, but his hurt feelings were all too real

I left without the power tool.

Over Christmas 2021, I watched several episodes of *Ramsay's Kitchen Nightmares* TV show. The chef visits failing restaurants, taste the food and points out why they are not successful. He swears a lot, is completely rude, and holds back no punches. It is trash TV. Or so I thought until I realised why I kept watching more episodes. The show at its heart is a life lesson about how to avoid failure by accepting personal responsibility. Once I noticed this, I enjoyed the episodes even more.

Each episode follows a certain format and has similar problems to solve. These are usually a mixture of poor quality food, poor customer service, obnoxious owners, unprofessional staff, a lack of hygiene, no clear management structure, no passion, and a sense of pending defeat. Gordon comes along and sparks fly as individuals are held accountable.

The issues are never technical or specialised. Gordon never points out that table clothes should be made of Egyptian cotton, but that they should be clean. He never says that frozen food cannot be used, but that it should not be advertised as fresh. He never complains that a dish is too simplistic, only that is it of poor quality.

The excuses start the second he walks into the restaurant. The owners blame the customers. The staff blame the owners for not listening. The chefs blame the owners for poor quality products or dictating the menu. Waiting staff blame a lack of organisation. Customers blame the quality of the food. No one mentions the dirt, grime and unhygienic practices until Gordon points them out.

The real issue in every restaurant is always a lack of personal responsibility by the owners. All other issues stem from this one problem. No one takes responsibility to ensure the kitchen and dining area are cleaned to an acceptable standard. No one is in charge of quality control as food leaves the kitchen. No one takes responsibility for staff morale or holds failing staff accountable. Owners portray themselves as the victims of the situation, the idea that they are ultimately in charge does not seem to cross their minds.

Except for a couple of infamous episodes, Gordon manages to turn around the restaurant by getting back to basics and forcing the owners to accept responsibility by fixing the problems. If the problem is a chef who will not change then the owner has to sack them. If the problem is filth everywhere then the owner has to put in place a cleaning regime. If the problem is a lack of organisation then the owner has to learn to be more organised. If the problem is the poor quality of food then the owner has to stop lying to themselves that the food is wonderful. Absolutely everything comes down to the owners accepting responsibility for everything in their restaurant.

I recommend everyone to watch a few of these episodes on YouTube to see how people resist accepting responsibility and any blame for the predicament they find themselves in. They blind themselves to reality and never self reflect on their performance as a leader or restaurateur. They seek out excuses of how it is not their fault but everyone else's. Some openly lie to Gordon which is caught on camera and then later exposed – lies become normal when they are a daily occurrence to one's self. It may be the only way they have managed to cope as their business slowly dies. Denial is the dish of the day until Gordon rips it apart to expose the rot. It is very painful for the individuals involved and even for us to watch sometimes, but it is always for the best.

A painful reality is always better than a painful unreality, at least with reality you can influence it with action.

Liberty means responsibility. That is why most men dread it.
- George Bernard Shaw

The call now is for each of us to ask ourselves: are we doing all we can to help build the country of our dreams?

- Nelson Mandela

Chapter 8

The Antidote

It is easy to criticise and point to problems, yet offer no solution. It is easy to read this book and think you are not part of the problem for you understand the issue and are anti woke. The truth is we all have to take some responsibility for the situation we are in as a country. None of us has done enough to push back against the tide of the 'nanny state' – in fact, most of us have promoted it. To be pampered from cradle to grave sounds amazing until you realise the cost you must pay and the fact that it is undeliverable.

This chapter outlines where we must push back to stop future generations from being sucked into a life of dependency resulting in the life of a beggar. We need to be administering tough love, promoting masculinity, creating more active fathers, offering a decent state education, reforming the welfare system, highlighting employment as more than just a wage, and finally, showing people the folly of having a victim mentality warped by woke ideology. *Dead easy*

The antidote to our problem is within you, within all of us. We are the solution to the making of a beggar. The first thing to ensure is that you are not one. If the issue we face is a negative mind virus then the solution is a positive mind virus. We need to figure out how we infect the people around us with this positive virus. As well as the person sitting next to you on the bus, and the individual who brushes past you on a busy street. How do we make our positive mind virus go airborne? How do we copy the Chinese and create an infection that rips through society and changes the population's behaviour? How do we develop a vaccine to combat the negative mind virus? Could it be a mixture of an annual shot of personal responsibility, washing your hands clean of the welfare state, and shaming people that are a danger to you and society?

I remember a chat with a man who had previously lived on the streets, he told me how a Hollywood movie changed his life for the better by following the one simple message of the film. The messenger was Jim Carrey, a comedian from films such as Ace Ventura: Pet Detective, The Truman Show and The Mask. One of his lesser-known films from his long list of endeavours is *Yes Man* from 2008. A simple story of a man who decides to say 'Yes' to every opportunity that comes his way to see if his life improves. It does. This former homeless man told me he watched the film on TV in a homeless hostel one evening when he felt really low and was considering going back onto the streets. He decided to copy the film's main character and start to say 'Yes' to opportunities being offered to him to see if his life would improve. It did. When I met him he had his own one-bedroom flat, a job, friends and a purpose in his life. He explained that it was not easy constantly saying 'Yes,' putting himself in uncomfortable situations, and constantly pushing himself, but it worked out. He said the hardest lesson to learn was that mistakes were still going to be made and negative consequences incurred. But on balance, a lot more positive outcomes came his way than negative ones. It was not a foolproof strategy, but a better one than he had ever had before.

Promote Tough Love

I have spent the last two decades administering tough love. Not a form of S&M or kink, but giving individuals the unvarnished truth they do not want to hear so they are prepared to take on the challenges of life. Without the truth, you are not present in reality. You are a visitor to a make-believe world where the truth is inconsequential, rejected as false, or perverted to fit a specific narrative. You become Alice through the looking glass.

I spent many years 'telling off kids' for their poor behaviour in the local community. Police officers and other partner agencies would refer individuals to me who were causing low-level issues. More serious issues were dealt with by official enforcement action. Rather than wait until a kid had crossed an invisible line to punish them, my job was to intervene much earlier to stop them from ever crossing that line. I worked with thousands of kids, the project was very successful.

I was good at it because I had been one of these kids and knew bullshit when I heard it. I saw my younger self in every child I spoke to. I wanted them to avoid the mistakes I had made by offering them the advice and guidance I never received. My job was to introduce them to their personal responsibility and show them the future consequences of their actions. I wanted every single one of them to be more than they imagined they could be. To facilitate this aim I came down on them hard, very hard.

> *I don't care how this makes you feel toward me. You may hate my guts, but I love you, and I am doing this because I love you.*
> **- Bill Milliken**

I would write to the parents of the child referred to me. I would invite the parents and child to the local police station for an informal chat. A 99% attendance rate showed that the parents cared about the future of their child – as it should be. I can count on one hand how many parents I met who gave the impression that they did not care about their child's future. I remember one single mum who was a self-confessed heroin addict and suspected prostitute. Her son's behaviour was a problem, he was going down the wrong path fast. We did not have much time before we thought he would cross the line – some kids just explode onto the scene, others grow with time. She broke down in tears and admitted that she was failing as a mum and knew it. She said she loved her son dearly and wanted him to have a better life than hers – she just did not know how to achieve it. Even *smackheads* love their children and want the best for them. A parent's love is a powerful thing if directed correctly. Once a parent was onboard, the rest of the journey was usually fairly easy. For this particular mum, I arranged for one-2-one parenting support for her to learn how to set boundaries and enforce rules. Things must have improved for this family as I never came across the kid's name again.

Some parents would arrive in a defensive state of mind. *I had the wrong kid. Their child never lies. Someone has it in for them.* I heard every excuse under the sun. In a few cases, the kid had the wrong attitude which never ended well for them. In both scenarios, I had to cut through the stalemate fast, these 'chats' were not debates. I would explain that if they lived in social housing we would evict the whole family if the behaviour continued. I would make it clear that the child would be responsible for the whole family losing their home. When mothers broke down and cried (95% of parents who attended were mothers), I would make the child look at their mother and apologise for hurting the person who loves them the most in the world. I had an answer for every situation. The vast majority of parents thanked me for bringing the issues to their attention, it gave them the information they needed to be more effective parents. Over 90% of the kids I saw once I never saw again, some came back for some more. Very silly.

Why was I so hard on them? I wanted the best for them in life. Doing what you want, when you want, does not lead you down the path to success, it leads you to a life of pain. I was trying to stop children from making mistakes that could ruin the rest of their lives. I was trying to stop a butterfly from flapping its wings and affecting a life not yet lived.

The prevention and early intervention of problems are better for everyone involved. Enforcement action takes a long time, is expensive and usually cannot be stopped once started. Early intervention is better for the individual for it gives them a chance to correct their ways and avoid mistakes that can have long-lasting effects. Prevention is better for the whole community for it reduces the number of victims of low-level antisocial behaviour. Quality of life issues is a priority for residents. Plus, it is also a lot cheaper than locking people up further down the road.

Let me tell you a true story of a woman who lost everything because of a brick, an ordinary house brick. It was a Friday evening. This lady and her husband were enjoying a nice quiet night at home in front of the TV. The living room window suddenly imploded as a brick crashed through it. Luckily, the curtains were drawn so they stopped the brick from flying across the room. Who threw the brick? Did they have enemies? The simple answer was that a local group of kids thought it would be funny and dared each other to do it.

This incident affected this woman tremendously. It shredded her nerves. She could not relax. Her doctor put her on medication. She got worse. Every noise, every sound scared her. When was the next brick going to come through the window? Her relationship with her husband suffered, and they start to argue. A year later he left. She was now on her own and more terrified than before.

The doctor increased her medication. She could not face going to work anymore in case her home was attacked again. Her sick record became unmanageable – she was dismissed. Her mortgage company did all they could but after 6 months of no payments, she was evicted. Within 18 months, this lady went from a happy life with a husband, her own house and a good job, to single, unemployed and homeless. All because a brick came through her window one Friday evening for no apparent reason.

When people criticise me for my tough-love approach, I explain how I am trying to not only improve the lives of the kids in front of me, but also the quality of life of the invisible victims of crimes that have not yet happened. I know this sounds a little like *Minority Report* – maybe it is. But we must never forget the truly innocent victims of crime.

Tough love is one of the ways we educate other people, especially children, for they do not have the experience needed to call upon when making decisions and choices. Many mammals practise such 'tough love' in the form of physical punishment towards their offspring as a way to teach them what they cannot do. We do the same when we smack a child for running across a road or using bad language. It should come as no surprise that this form of parental punishment is under threat from the same governments that are turning us into beggars. It is already illegal in Scotland and Wales to smack your child. Let me be clear, beating the crap out of your child is not smacking, it is child abuse and is already illegal. But the short, sharp shock of being smacked on the bum, or the hand, sends an immediate signal to the child that whatever they were doing was wrong and will not be tolerated. A tough lesson from a place of love.

Telling people things they do not want to hear is difficult, but what other option do you have if you care about them? What would you do if your friend had a body odour problem? Ignore it? Let them go through life not understanding why they are not popular, why they cannot get a date? If they knew they smelt they would do something about it, but they do not, so they cannot. The caring thing to do is to tell them. You will feel uncomfortable and potentially nasty, but doing nothing benefits no one and does harm. Tough love can be tough on the person dishing it out - unless they are a psychopath.

We need more tough love in our society, administered by society. Not just directed at children, but directed towards everyone for we all need it at different times of our life. We need to tell people the truth if their actions, decisions or lifestyle choices are harmful to them or society. We need to call out individuals who are parasites, race-baiters, conmen and beggars. Compassion is the emotion we use to infantilise others for our own convenience and peace of mind. We lie and tell ourselves that we do not want to hurt their feelings, whereas the reality is that we do not want to feel uncomfortable and have to deal with an emotional roller-coaster.

We need to stop our national pastime of trying not to upset anyone. We need to stop lying to people by telling them that their lifestyle is as valid and as valuable as any other. For they are not, some are definitely better than others. We need to stop telling individuals that they are good enough as they are, for they are not, they can be better. Our focus on validating the choices of individuals is not helpful. We should allow all adults to make the choices they wish, but we should be educating them on the best option for them and society. But the choice should always be theirs.

How do you know what you are capable of achieving if you are never in a position to challenge yourself? *Cometh the hour, cometh the man*. My cancellation in 2020 showed me that I was braver and more formidable than I truly believed. Like all boys, I have pretended many times that I would be a hero in the right situation, knowing deep down inside that I would be a coward like everyone else. But when my life was ruined and I faced injustice, I fought the fight of my life and surprised everyone with the result. It would have been easier for me to stay curled up in a ball and slowly die. I had to give myself a good talking to if I was to ever get out of the dark place I found myself in. I needed to find the strength to fight, surprisingly, it was just sitting there waiting to be needed.

Everything I do and say comes from a place of love. I want the best for you and the rest of my country. I promote tough love messages because someone has to be the adult in the room and point out the facts, otherwise 'the kids' will set fire to the place just to see what happens. Life is not a series of wonderful experiences, it is a series of common-sense decisions if you want to keep the life you are accustomed to. To achieve more requires hard work, dedication and some luck.

Tough love does not produce beggars, it produces personal responsibility.

Promote Masculinity

A society needs a balance of masculinity and femininity. Yin and yang. Light and darkness. Order and chaos. One option is not better than the other, we need both to work together in harmony. Currently, the pendulum has swung too far towards femininity. We are seeing the over feminisation of society, this is beneficial to no one.

This can be seen by the plethora of words and phrases that are thrown around on social media: be kind, tolerant, compassionate, diverse, inclusive, black lives matter, and climate emergency. They all evoke emotion. They do not foster debate, argument or the use of facts.

Inclusivity is the new mantra. It means we should allow everyone and everything to be involved in our life, our community and society. There can be no judging other people's choices, culture or beliefs, for this is bigotry and prejudicial. We are all God's creatures and we are all equal. We know this is not true. It is the same mantra from mothers of small children. *Play nicely. Share your toys. Don't be rude.* These social lessons are important for children to be socialised and to make friends. But they are not helpful when applied to a whole society in a complicated multi-faceted world.

If you want to understand what masculinity has done to benefit you then look out of the nearest window. What do you see? It does not matter what you can see, for I know it was all invented by men, designed by men, built by men and maintained by men. Men created the modern world for the benefit of everyone. The weaker and poorer you are, the more you have benefited. The one thing men are missing from all this work is the gratitude they are owed, especially from a small group of women – aka feminists. A simple thank you would suffice – for you are welcome and men will continue to do more for you to enjoy.

Boys are penalised for not being girls. The UK education system is designed for girls, run by women, and achieves the best results for females. Boys' needs are ignored at best, or actively punished at worse. They are constantly compared to girls and found wanting - for they are not girls. Their natural high-energy and related behaviour is frowned upon and punished. They are constantly told '*Why can't you be more like the girls?.*' And we wonder why they are failing, confused and angry.

We need to allow boys to be boys. For example, we need to kick girls out of the *Scouts* and have opportunities for boys to learn what it is to be a man surrounded by other males. They do not need to be judged by girls in an environment that was created especially for them. Boys need their own space. I do not wish to stop girls from doing what *Scouts* do, they just need to set up their own organisation to do it. Females need to stop appropriating existing male organisations with screams of equality.

We need to start promoting masculinity as a positive and challenge all attempts to brand it as toxic. We need to bring back male-only spaces for this is where men can be men, learn from one another, and be held accountable if they fall short. Men act differently when women are around, they do not portray their true selves. Women are currently understanding how it feels to lose their single-sex spaces, it is a shame they never spoke out when men were losing theirs.

Men and boys toughen each other up. It may not be pleasant to watch, but it is the way we prepare each other for life and everything it throws at us. We give each other rude and insulting nicknames, this prepares us for worse in the future. We 'take the mickey' out of each other, we point out each other's mistakes, we are ruthless and cruel. But this bonds us together, gives us resilience, pushes us to do better, and prepares us for the ridicule of trying and failing. Over time it creates a hierarchy or a pecking order, everyone knows their place in the group. This reduces the need for violence and confrontation, it has all been sorted out naturally. Individuals who do not like the outcome leave the group and seek another to join. Grudges are not held. Men can bump into one another after several decades of no contact and start exactly where they left off.

We have become so feminised as a nation that we now try to remedy male problems by using female solutions. The best example of this is male suicide prevention. We are told that '*if only men would talk about their feelings and problems*' they would not kill themselves at three times the rate of women. If I had to talk about my feelings and problems, I would want to kill myself. I cannot think of something more degrading than laying my problems out so I can chat about them with a friend. Problems are there to be solved, not discussed. Male suicide has nothing to do with the inability of sharing problems. Women talk about their problems all the time, yet they 'try' to kill themselves at a higher rate than men. The self-reported happiness of women has fallen relative to that of men since the 1950s, so whatever they are doing is not working (https://www.dailymail.co.uk/femail/article-1189894/Women-happy-years-ago-.html). An ironic difference between men and women when it comes to suicide is that women are rubbish at it, they try and fail. When a man puts his mind to something he succeeds – 16 men a day in just England and Wales.

This brings us into the field of mental health, the new 'bad back' of excuses. For many decades lazy individuals would claim to have a bad back to avoid work, to get time off work, or simply not to work at all. It was a great excuse for it could not be proven one way or another, but advancements in science and medicine eventually put a stop to such claims. Stating you have a mental health condition is the new acceptable way to dismiss your personal responsibility. It excuses your poor behaviour, allows you to attract sympathy and advertises you as a 'special victim' of circumstance.

The huge increase in mental health conditions over the last 30 years makes no sense to me. Life is now easier. We have everything we think we need, yet we have an increase in reported mental health issues. It is as if the success of our society has a damaging effect. Or more likely, that we have removed so many problems and issues that people do not know what to worry over, so have to subconsciously make up problems to fill a gap. Good examples are racism, gender confusion, climate emergency and misogamy. The state of one's mental health is a non-political excuse from weak individuals who are looking to others to make concessions to them. The more we discuss and accept the need to normalise mental health issues, the more people fall into the trap. Anxiety and depression are not mental health problems. It is your subconscious telling you something is wrong and you need to make changes. But for decades, we have given people medication to dampen down these warnings. Pills are seen as the answer but no one gets better. Instead of medication, we need to create resilience within people so they can spot the warning signs that something may be wrong and have the confidence to fix their problems. The more a mental health condition is highlighted, the more people are convinced they suffer from it. It is learnt behaviour that is currently rewarded in our society with empathy, pity and attention.

A term I like and use is *'man up.'* It is exactly what we need to do as a country. It means to take responsibility and stop moaning. If something needs doing then get it done. If you have been treated unfairly then get over it. If you are not happy with your life then change it. If you hate your job then do something about it. Men cannot respect other men who are weak, pathetic and whinny, for these men will not have your back when the barbarian horde is at the gate. *'Man up'* is a two-word training programme for men who have failed to be all they can be in the eyes of other men. It is a reminder they are better than their current state and need to do something about it. Men instinctively know what it means and what they need to do – whether they do it or not is another matter.

We need to stop women from using the slur of the invisible 'patriarchy' to pretend that women are persecuted and dominated in society. The facts do not bear this out for women are flourishing in our society. You can make an argument that this success is at the detriment of men – but you do not hear men complaining and moaning about it. If there is such a thing as the patriarchy and tyrannical men are trying to keep women in their place, then these men are not doing a very good job for women are doing great – good for them. This excuse from specific women to explain their underachievement does not make any sense in the UK. Even historically men did not hold women back, it was mother nature that held women back. Men developed the technology to free women from the constraints of unpredictable and constant pregnancy. Men eliminated infant mortality and made the streets safe to walk for the weaker sex. Men created an environment for women to flourish, and flourish they did. But somewhere along the way amnesia set in and we all forgot how women got to where they are today. We think it has something to do with a woman jumping in front of the King's horse or others handcuffing themselves to railings a hundred years ago. The emancipation of women happened everywhere technology was embraced. There was no need for female civil disobedience for there was no patriarchal evil power suppressing women, large parts of the population were suppressed regardless of sex. Remember that when eight million women got the vote for the first time in 1918, five million work-class men also got the vote on the same day. Most of these men were still on the continent as WWI had ended the month before and it took a long time to repatriate all the soldiers. It is insulting to think that men singled out women for unfair treatment, for nature picked out the vast majority of people for unfair treatment. The real difference between the sexes is that men took on nature and beat it to benefit us all.

Finally, let us stop telling men to accept being less than they know they should be, we need to demand better from men for it is better for them. Let us show boys what real men have achieved throughout history and that we expect them to carry on this role of protector and provider of society. They have the potential to be future legends and heroes - boys know this to be true for many of their games revolve around such fantasies. If we can tap into this innate desire then we can produce a generation of men that are striving and competing to serve society for the benefit of all. Tonic masculinity.

Masculinity does not produce beggars, it produces self-respect.

Promote Fatherhood

Children need fathers. Adults need fathers. Functioning societies need fathers.

Fathers bring many benefits to a child's life, they are a crucial factor in the development of both boys and girls. They are not, and should not be, in competition with mothers to discover who is the best parent. Fathers are equally valuable and needed, they bring different things to the table. As it should be and is designed to be. Parents are a team. Parenting is a game for two, you can play it solo but it is not optimal for anyone involved.

How does a boy discover what a man is without watching and engaging with his father on a daily basis? How does a girl discover the acceptable way to be treated by a man without engaging with her father? They both watch how he works in partnership with their mother to understand relationships, comprise and raise a family.

Fathers bring order to a family. Raising children is hard work and was designed to be done by two people, not one. Men want to be fathers, we should not only allow them to be, but we should be promoting it as an honour, a privilege, a duty. They are not an extra feature or add-on.

Mothers are good at protecting their children from immediate danger, that is why females instinctively pick up babies, it removes them from ground level and predators. Fathers prepare children for the dangers they are sure to encounter throughout life. There is a difference in parenting roles, both are equally important.

Fathers love to 'toy fight' with their children. It is not only a bonding exercise that fosters trust, but an essential part of a child's development to understand their body. They figure out how far they can bend without breaking, how hard they can get hit without it hurting, and what level of aggression is not acceptable. It shows them they are not easily broken or damaged. All valuable lessons for a growing child that helps to build resilience, confidence and empathy.

When a father's influence is ignored, rejected or dismissed, the love of a mother can become too much. *Too controlling. Too overbearing. Too protective.* We have a new term for such mothers. A *helicopter parent* is one that pays extremely close attention to a child's experiences and problems – they are nearly all mothers. They are so named because they 'hover around' and are constantly watching every aspect of their child's life, including strictly managing social interactions and friendships.

The term has been in use since the late 1980s. It gained wider circulation when American academic administrators began using it in the early 2000s when the parent role seemingly changed and parents started to phone up university professors to complain about their child's grades. At the same time, some students admitted their parents phone them up every morning to get them out of bed - part of this change in behaviour is down to technology. The mobile phone has been called *'the world's longest umbilical cord.'*

As these students graduated and entered the workforce, companies reported *helicopter parents* showing up in the workplace. Phoning managers to advocate on their adult child's behalf or to negotiate salaries. There is a similar trend in China called *Tiger Mothers.* Their emphasis is on hard work with parents adopting an extreme, rigid and authoritarian approach to ensure success. This is in contrast to western *helicopter parents* who coddle their children and crave their friendship.

One of the roles of fathers is one that no one wants to admit is a problem, the protection of a child from its mother. Let us skip over the physical abuse that can be administered by a mother and look at the emotional damage that can be done. *Mother's nurture.* It is innate in nearly all mothers. But what happens when this nurturing goes too far, becomes overbearing and suffocates the child's development? This is where the father steps in. When a mother stops her child from climbing a tree in case they get hurt – a father steps in. When a mother tells her child that outside is dangerous and it is safer to stay home – a father steps in. When a mother tells her son that no woman is good enough for him and he should stay with her forever – a father steps in.

A parent's job is to raise their child to adulthood with the skills to be independent and then to release them into the wild to cope by themselves, and ultimately to be successful. Job over. If your adult child cannot cope in the real world then you have failed as a parent, for you have set them up to be a burden on others and a disappointment to themselves. The more a father is involved, the less likely for this to happen.

There are many benefits an active father brings to the lives of his children, here are just a few:

- **For fun**. Fathers like to be physical, roll around on the floor and 'toy fight' with their children. Kids love this type of play and it can be used as a reward for good behaviour. It helps children to develop coordination, build confidence and understand how much force is appropriate to use.

- **For balance**. Kids benefit from being exposed to different opinions, personalities and parenting styles. Parents have different strengths, weaknesses and points of view, this prepares children for a world where everyone is different.

- **To understand men**. For kids to understand the role of a man they have to see male role models in the home, the best role model is always the father. Boys need to see their future selves, girls need to see their future husbands.

- **For behaviour**. Fathers tend to be more firm and fair when it comes to discipline, this leads to better outcomes for the kids for their behaviour is better over the long term. *Wait till your father gets home!*

- **For education**. Kids with active fathers do better in education. Not just at school, but also before school where they learn social skills and language. They also develop higher IQs.

- **For friendships**. Kids with involved fathers develop better social skills and therefore have stronger friendships with less conflict. They are better at giving and sharing with other children.

- **For mental health**. Kids who have an active father have lower incidences of depression, suicide, self-harm and other mental health problems.

- **For self-esteem**. Gaining the love and attention of your father increases a kid's sense of self-worth.

- **For confidence**. Fathers tend to push kids to do more and do better. They encourage them to take acceptable risks and chances.

- **For future relationships**. Kids who have a good relationship with both parents are more likely to have successful relationships when older. Fathers show their sons how to treat a woman and they show their daughters how to expect to be treated.

- **For security.** Kids feel safer with a father around and are usually better at dealing with being teased or bullied. They are also usually better off financially which leads to stable home life.

- **For morality.** Kids with a strong positive relationship with their father have a lower risk of becoming criminals, abusing alcohol or drugs, and making poor choices.

- **For wisdom.** Fathers have a lot of experience and life skills to pass on to their children. They offer advice and guidance to help them to understand life and avoid problems.

- **For future career**. Kids with active fathers gain better jobs.

- **For happiness**. Fathers make kids happy.

In some families the father is not available for different reasons, he may have died, be in prison or left the country. This is where grandads and other male family members come in to play. A father is irreplaceable, but a family substitute is better than no male role model at all.

As a fairly new grandad, I am constantly told off by my wife for teasing our granddaughter. She is lucky she has a great dad, I am just an additional male role model. I am accused of being mean and trying to upset our little cherub. Nothing could be further from the truth. I am challenging my granddaughter to understand that not all situations will go in her favour. That some people will take her belongings and individuals will be a pain in the arse. She reacts to me with love and affection for she gets all my attention when we are together. She does not realise I am educating her to be ready for the real world. For most of the time I have spent with her I did not realise I was doing such a thing - I thought I was just playing with her. But while writing this book, I realised why I was doing what I was doing. I want her to be resilient, strong-minded, capable and in control of her emotions. I am making a difference in her life and she will love me forever. I was the first person she walked to. The first person she puckered up and kissed, and the first person she said she missed when I was not there.

Fathers are different. They do things their way. It is no better nor worse than a mother's way. It is just a different way.

Fathers do not produce beggars, they produce resilient individuals.

Promote Productive Education

We need a practical education system that prepares young people for what is expected of them in life. What has destroyed our education system is progressivism, now called *wokeness*. We discarded what we knew to work, for a new way that makes everyone feel special inside. Sports day with no winners. Games where no one keeps score. Celebration events where everyone gets a certificate. Classrooms where tables do not face the front of the class, but other pupils because they are in control of their own learning. The only thing missing is 'group hugs' and a chorus of *kumbaya*.

The ultimate aim of our state-funded education system should be to prepare the next generation for an adult working life to pay their way in the world. I know some people will disagree with me and say that learning is in itself the aim and reward – foolish nonsense for the vast majority of kids. I have never met an unemployed teenager whose ability to recite Shakespearian sonnets is a comfort to them when claiming unemployment benefits on a council estate.

After eleven years of state-funded compulsory education, why do we have a significant number of pupils who are unemployable? Dysfunctional and unable to read and write at a basic level? The UK budget for education is approx £100 billion per year, this covers all aspects. Many pupils do well in our education system which is great news. But life's future beggars do not do well in our tax-funded school system. They are failed by a system that is designed as a one-size-fits-all. The failure is not just the school's fault. They are also failed by their parents for not demanding better, and by themselves for rejecting their personal responsibility.

According to the former Schools Minister, Nick Gibb MP, in July 2015 when he addressed the *Education Reform Summit,* he stated the three main aims of our education system are to empower young people to succeed in the economy, participate in culture, and leave school prepared for adult life. I would say lots of schools are failing many pupils based on the government's own success metric.

In November 2017, the ex-UCAS chief, Mary Curnock Cook, who was head of the university admissions service until 2016, stated her alarm that boys falling behind at school had become '*normalised,*' also that this conversation was now '*taboo*' because of feminist pressure groups. She said: "*In about ten years' time the gap between boys and girls will be worse than rich and poor. That is astonishing really.*"

Girls outperform boys in every year of education. They get better GCSE and A level results. More females go to university and they get better grades. This success is not simply handed to them, I am sure they have to work hard to achieve, but the system is slanted in their favour for it rewards feminine character traits. Nearly every beggar I have ever met on the streets failed at school. Unsurprisingly, every criminal I have worked with also failed education. 99% of them were men.

Why do we not place our hand into a red hot fire? Why do we not touch the water inside a boiling kettle? Because we know it will be painful, there will be a negative consequence to accept for this action. We do not want the pain, so we do not do what we know will result in pain. The fact that the negative consequence is instantaneous is a huge deterrent. Our body generates pain to tell us that whatever we are doing is harmful and to stop – it punishes us in the hope we will learn not to do it again. That is the job of pain. Tough love.

Corporal punishment has the same effect if administered correctly. Animals use their version of this type of 'learning' very successfully. I noticed a deterioration of discipline in schools when corporal punishment was banned in schools in 1986. The deterrent to control poor behaviour became staying after school in detention or informing parents of the behaviour. These sanctions do not have the same level of intimidation and fear attached, plus they are not instantaneous. I appreciate that some teachers historically went overboard in administering punishments – I saw it with my own eyes. But all this can be rectified with new technology, procedures and training. (I also think we should look at a new capital punishment system for a modern world – but this is a discussion for another day.)

Pupils can learn very quickly how to behave, not because they are punished but because the threat of punishment is there and will be used. Just like the hot kettle scenario, young people comprehend that their actions can have negative consequences for them, especially in the here and now. They take this learning into adult life and continue to think through actions to highlight negative consequences. This is a vital skill that helps us to avoid mistakes that could potentially ruin us. I have worked with many young people who were in trouble with the police because they could not think ahead. They never saw the obvious consequence of their action. How can a life of no consequences teach you to be careful and thoughtful? It does not.

Bullying in schools is not a problem - the idea that we need to do more about bullying in schools is the problem. Children are little evil devils, they are born that way. They have to be civilised by parents, school and the community. But to think we can stop nasty people from being nasty is preposterous for we cannot, especially in the age of social media. All that happens is we undermine the social development of the child being bullied and we make them a victim. We remove the opportunity for them to remedy the situation by walking away, sticking up for themselves or smacking the other kid in the mouth. Running to an authority figure to report the issue only produces weak individuals who are not prepared for the real world. We have bullies everywhere in society and the sooner we learn how to deal with them the better. Studies have shown that children who are bullied are much more likely to be bullied by others in adult life. Their weakness is spotted by nasty individuals and the abuse starts. Being bullied has very little to do with your physical characteristics, the problem is a personal demeanour that flags you as easy prey. We should use bullying in school as a valuable learning opportunity for us to overcome so we are prepared to deal with it later in life.

University use to be the pinnacle of our educational journey. Only the best and brightest attended. Today it is a financial racket to make money off the poor and stupid. All subsidised by the taxpayer who foots the bill for the vast majority of student loans. The government loans out £20 billion per year to approx 1.5 million students, with the expectation that 25% of loans will be paid back in full. Universities are making money hand over fist.

A friend of mine from Twitter, **@HeadWarriorTWM**, explains the problem with universities in a simple succinct way. *"University students are now just customers, they use to be the product."* When the quality of your product declines, there will be a reckoning – eventually.

To enable more and more people to attend university, courses have been watered down. Some have even been created just for individuals who cannot get onto other courses. A flavour of some of the silly courses available, or were recently available, in the UK: *Surf Science and Technology, Floral Design, Hand Embroidery, Psychology of Fashion, Puppetry Design and Performance, Stand-Up Comedy*. I have no problem with individuals studying what they wish, but the taxpayer should not be subsidising worthless courses.

Then we have the damaging courses which indoctrinate, brainwash and sow the seeds of the destruction of our way of life. These courses have no science behind them, only ideology. Courses include

Women's Studies, Gender Studies, Black Studies, and *Queer Studies*.

The *American Pew Research Center* 2019 survey found that the more education a black person receives, the more likely they are to say they experience regular racism. This figure is nearly twice as much when you compare university graduates to non-graduates, 9% compared to 17%. Does this mean you have to be clever to spot racism directed at you? Or is the simpler answer that universities have trained students to be hyper-sensitive about race and therefore they see racism everywhere. Hence the terms micro-aggression, institutional racism, and white privilege. After four years of higher education, we produce adults who are convinced they are victims, that society is out to get them, and the cards are stacked against them. Mind-boggling stupidity. We call it indoctrination.

An article from July 2021 in the *Evening Standard*, stated findings from the latest graduate outcomes survey by the *Higher Education Statistics Agency*. Of young people leaving university in 2018/19, just over half (56%) of UK-domiciled graduates were in full-time employment around 15 months after finishing their courses, compared with 59% of the 2017/18 cohort. Is this success? Why are they not all in well-paid jobs? Or has university become the production of well-educated beggars?

Good education does not produce beggars, it produces thinkers.

Promote The Dangers Of Welfare

Our welfare state system needs to be a 'hand-up' system, not a 'handout' system. We need a welfare system, I am not an abolitionist, I am a reformer.

Every successful person in the world had help and support along the way. No one achieves success by themselves, it is virtually impossible. This is why we are social animals and designed to live in tribes for we cannot be successful without others around us. This is essentially what the welfare state is, a larger more comprehensive version of the support a tribe offers to its members. And I for one want a welfare state – just not the one we have.

A safety net is a device to protect people from injury when falling from a height. It achieves this by reducing the distance the person falls and dissipating the energy of the impact. They are used by circus acts who perform their feats of entertainment way up high on tightropes. If they fall their show may be ruined but at least they live to try again. We also use this phrase to describe our welfare system for its job is to catch people who fall in life so they do not hit the bottom of society. It aims to minimise the impact of such a fall and get them back on their feet so they can try again. It is a fair analogy.

A married couple with two young children may have a good life, but what happens when the father is killed in a car accident? Do we allow this family to try to cope on their own? Lose their home and become homeless? No. Of course, we do not. The welfare state steps in and offers help and support to compensate for an unforeseen accident. There is an argument that they should have personal insurance for such an accident – but let us not worry about this here. Do we fund the State to come to their aid out of kindness? I do not believe we do. We do it to stop us from feeling uncomfortable if we have to look at real poverty and deprivation in the future. We do it because it ultimately benefits us, and this is where the problem lies. We are trying to make ourselves feel better, rather than improve the lives of the 'so called' unfortunate.

A safety net is designed to catch you if you make a big mistake or have some bad luck. It is not a destination of choice. It should not be somewhere people are throwing themselves into as an acceptable goal. Hitting the safety net means you have failed in your current quest, it does not mean you make it your home. When a circus performer hits the net they are ashamed for they know they can do better. They climb out of the net and signal an apology to the crowd who did not come along to see failure.

Our safety net has become a fishing net. A huge commercial trawling net that is dragged through communities and captures people with no way of escape. We do not use a rod and bait to find exactly what we are hoping to catch for this is too simplistic.

We need to stop rewarding poor choices. This will be a tough lesson for some already in the system, but it will help those who have not yet made poor choices. Failing education, criminal record, single parenthood, face tattoos, morbidly obese and many others. We need to nudge people towards the best path for them to be successful. The choice is theirs to make for I do not want the State to remove personal responsibility. But if the choices are not conducive to the expectations of taxpayers then penalties need to be applied. *You take our money, you follow our rules.*

We know incentives work on people. This is why some companies give out employee bonuses or link pay raises to productivity – it makes most of us work a little harder. This is a valuable lesson our welfare system could be imparting to claimants. Nudging them to work a little harder in finding a job. How this would work I do not know for I have not given it enough thought, but I know we do respond to positive incentives. How about a small bonus for every job interview attended or a bonus if a job is secured within the first two months of becoming unemployed. These are quick examples to give you an idea, I have not given them more than 20 seconds of thought.

I also know we respond to negative incentives. Claiming unemployment benefit is more challenging than when I use to claim many decades ago. I use to go on holiday to Spain, come back with a suntan, be days late to sign on, and just say I was ill – no problem at all. Today you would lose your payment. If we accept that claiming unemployment benefits is a temporary situation, then should payments be reduced over time? Should the individual attend all appointments dressed as if it was a job interview? Should claimants be forced to take any job on offer or volunteer to gain skills? Do we write off many of these people for they are too long in the tooth and will not change? Do we start a new system for younger people so they do not end up thinking the safety net is their ultimate destination? All complicated questions with no easy answers. But I feel we are not even asking questions anymore and are happy to keep paying people to do nothing with their lives for it is more convenient for us.

We live in a time of eco-green maniacs where everything needs to be recyclable and environmentally friendly. Except when it comes to us as individuals and our intrinsic worth. We are hardly ever recycled, we are just dumped into the benefits system to rot. Where are the campaigns and public protests to improve the life chances of welfare recipients? All we ever hear is that the system does not give enough free money to individuals. No one ever talks about the wasted lives while sitting on the dole. Every individual who is paid by us not to work is not fulfilling their destiny. They are not living their best life. Trapped in purgatory – neither heaven nor hell, just a waiting room – waiting for life to begin.

Part of the problem is that we have fallen for the idea that socialism is good and that the State needs to take care of us. Nothing could be further from the truth. The State should serve us, not rule over us. Let us look at socialism as an ideology, it is generally accepted that socialism caused the deaths of approx 100 million people last century. How? If you add up the deaths caused by Mao, Stalin and Hitler then you have a better understanding. Do not be surprised that Hitler is on this list of socialists for that is exactly what he was. Hitler spoke many times about his party of national socialists were the only true socialists. Even Mussolini was a lifelong socialist. It seems that all the bad people last century were socialists, is this true today? A discussion for another day perhaps.

It is not the role of the State to look after us as if we were children, for we are not. If we are children then the State has to make all our decisions for us – but we are not. Having the State running your life is something you do not want to happen for I have worked in government, I have seen the incompetence and waste. The vast majority of people will have a better life if they have less contact with the government. Doing the wrong thing for the right reason is still the wrong thing to do – welcome to government.

Our welfare system is too comfortable, too easy to access, and too socially acceptable to be within. Dependency is risky for it removes the power from you and gives it to another. It may feel safe and even be beneficial. But risk increases as dependency grows. Life is complicated, we do not know what is around the next corner. Placing your life in the hands of others is not a sensible strategy. A smart business never replies completely on just one customer or one income stream.

The Lord giveth and the Lord taketh away.
- The Bible, Job 1:21

A farmer protects his flock. He looks after them and ensures they are healthy. He spends his money to purchase food and vet services. He is their guardian, their master, their protector and provider. But eventually, he will come along with a stun gun and a butchering knife. A false sense of security is not the same as real security. Do not be fooled by handouts, they are never without cost or risk.

Our welfare system produces beggars, self-sufficiency does not.

Promote The Benefits Of Employment

If you do not work you have to rely on others to support you. You cannot pay your own way. You are a burden. You have a negative effect on society. You are a parasite - living in, on, or with another organism to obtain nutrients, grow, or multiply often in a state that directly or indirectly harms the host.

There are exceptions to the above. You may be retired or have savings. Your partner may be supporting the family so you can raise your children. Or you may be in a tiny percentage of disabled individuals who cannot perform simple actions. The vast majority of disabled people can work and should work - many already do. We should not write people off for our convenience, we should look at how we can support them into work and keep them there. We could remove the minimum wage requirements for employers to take on specific individuals if they are not as productive as others – the State would top up their wage to the minimum wage level. This would improve the quality of life for so many disabled people for they would be productive members of society, not sitting at home on benefits.

Immigration has been a double-edged sword. It is great for employers for they get a larger pool of people to choose from to fill their vacancies. They usually find better educated and more competent individuals. The downside is that an oversupply of job seekers pushes down wages. It stops the training of local people to fill vacancies. It also delays investment in technology that replace low skilled jobs with higher-skilled positions. If we want people to work we have to be fair in terms of the rate of pay. No one wants to go back to the days of poverty wages. The Left has fought too hard and for too long to go backwards.

No one can argue with the phrase: '*a decent day's pay for a decent day's work.*'

In some cases it is not the rate of pay that is the issue, it is the type of job on offer. We need to remove the unbelievable sense of entitlement that certain jobs are too lowly to accept. I have spoken to many young people who turn their noses up at the opportunity of employment because they perceive the job is beneath them. The phrase commonly used is '*only immigrants do that job.*' We hear the same type of statement all the time on TV when discussions around immigration are had. We are told that we need more immigration because British people will not do specific jobs, such as in the care sector. So we have to steal people from other countries to come here and do the jobs. No one asks why British people do not want such jobs because the answer is obvious. The job does not pay enough for the amount of work and stress involved. The simple answer is to increase the rate of pay for this role and more people will want to do it. A market economy only works if the government stops interfering in it. Bringing in more migrants only keeps wages low and pushes British people into the welfare trap.

If we have job vacancies in a local area and have unemployed individuals claiming benefits every fortnight, then we have a problem. Should we have local rules in place that reflect the reality on the ground? Job seeking in London is so much easier than in Lancashire.

Employment needs to be promoted as the expected norm in our society. Some will say that it is already expected in society, but it is definitely not promoted. The days of living off other people's hard work need to end. We need a twin-track approach highlighting the benefits of being in paid employment and the negative effects of choosing to be a beggar. We need to bring back societal shame.

What are the benefits of employment?

- Gives you a reason to get out of bed in the morning
- Gives you a sense of pride, respect and meaning
- Enables you to socialise and meet new friends
- Provides you with money to pay your way
- Increases your skills and knowledge
- Improves your mental health and well-being
- Increases your happiness due to sense of purpose
- Increases your security by having a reliable wage
- Increases your chance of finding a better-paid job
- Increases your self-esteem due to you paying your way

These benefits are personal to the individual. Not financial savings to the Exchequer, even though these will be massive. Especially if we take into account the reduced call upon other services, such as the criminal justice system, NHS and social services. We need to forget about the financial benefits to the government and sell the idea of employment as a plus for the individual. Currently, this is never attempted. I want individuals to have better and more fulfilling lives. I do not care if the government saves money, for they will only waste it elsewhere.

More working individuals lead to happier people. This leads to better neighbourhoods with less crime and this produces better citizens. This positive feedback loop is what we need to transform our communities.

Employment does not produce beggars, it produces self-respect.

Avoid Victim Mentality

This is better described as *excuse mentality*. It is tough to get up every day and face the realities of a world that does not care about you. It is tough to do better than you did yesterday. It requires hard work to be successful. Manufacturing an excuse to explain away all your failings and underachievement means you can stop trying to better yourself, for it is pointless.

A beggar is a victim by definition. Why else would they be begging and humiliating themselves in front of the world? Once you believe you are a victim, then you are a victim and therefore act like a victim. That is the trap of victim mentality, it opens the door to victimhood. A place where *'you can check out any time you like - but you can never leave!'* - a victim's *Hotel California*.

We need to stop thinking that the world owes us a living, that we are special, or that we are unfairly treated by life. For the truth be told, if you are in the UK then you are in the top 1% of luckiest people ever to be born in the history of the world. If you have a problem in the UK then it is probably a 'first world' problem, or you are the problem.

We need to stop talking about poverty for it creates a new set of 'so called' victims who believe they are unfortunate. Most importantly, we need to stop talking about poverty because we have none in the UK. Not if you mean children suffering from malnutrition, families living on the streets, or a lack of services such as health care and education.

There is no single, universally accepted definition of poverty, it changes depending on your agenda. The government uses this definition: *'people in relative low income – living in households with income below 60% of the median in that year.'* This definition equates to 20% of the UK today living in poverty. Silliness.

The only poverty we have in the UK is a poverty of aspiration, a lack of dreams, missing fathers, and the absence of self-belief. When people suffer in the UK, and they do, it is not because of a lack of free money or State support. It is because individuals make poor choices for themselves and their families. Correct these mistakes and the UK will reward you. We constantly give people chance after chance until one germinates, as it should be in a caring society.

The most harmful part of this mentality is once you believe you are a victim, you stop trying to improve your situation because you believe it to be hopeless. Hopelessness is a terrible mental disease and can be contagious. A lesson we need to teach in society is that it is never hopeless. Nothing is written in the stars, there is no overarching master plan for your life. You are an individual and are in charge of your destiny and future. Others can influence it and they surely do. But you should never relinquish control of your choices even if you think you have none to be made.

When feelings of hopelessness appear for they do visit everyone, combat them with your memories of overcoming adversaries which led to victory. We all have personal stories of being successful and achieving, they may seem inconsequential but they are not – they are evidence of you succeeding.

Almost everyone can be a victim in the UK today. If you are not white, not straight or not male then you are most definitely a victim of some sort of prejudice and bigotry according to the woke

- this is not up for discussion, according to the woke.

But do not worry if you are white, straight and male, there are many loopholes for you to use to gain your victim status. Are you a Gypsy or a traveller? Non-Christian? Disabled? Fat? Mental health issues? Learning difficulties? These are all 'so called' legitimate victim statuses in the UK. It is surprising that anything works in the country with so many weak and pathetic individuals crying into their cornflakes every morning.

We all know life is hard. It may not be as hard as it once was, but that is no consolation when you are struggling today. Your life may not seem as easy when compared to David Beckham or Elon Musk, but you have no real idea about their life, worries or problems. Michael Jackson and Prince both died of drug misuse to dampen down internal woes, looking from the outside their lives looked amazing.

Your only comparison should be with your life as it was yesterday, last month, or last year. Has it improved? If not what did you do wrong? What will you change?

A small percentage of women, aka feminists, need to stop moaning. Women have equality, their future is in their hands. But they have to stop blaming men and the patriarchy for their failures and personal underachievement. Women are either powerful and independent or weak and pathetic. They cannot on one hand say they are as capable as men, and then the next day say they need special laws to protect them. This is the question women need to answer: *do you want equal rights or special rights?* Equal rights mean you take all the 'crap' men have to deal with and still move forward. Special rights mean you get no 'crap' because men look after you. Take your pick.

If you are black and think the UK is racist then go and ask your parents or grandparents why they came here and what life was like in their homeland? Why do we have hundreds of thousands of foreigners wanting to come to the UK and make it their home? Why do virtually no migrants ever go back home once they settle here? You need to find answers to these questions instead of listening to race-baiters who sell you a false reality. You have been lied to by people who wish you use your naivety and anger as a political tool to further their own agenda. Stop wasting the wonderful opportunity your family gave you by moving here to make their home. They wanted to give you all the opportunities this amazing country has on offer. Any disappointment in your life is of your making.

The LGBTQ+ *'alphabet people'* have no reason to complain whatsoever. Sometimes it feels like it is almost mandatory for you to be gay or one of the many subsidiaries of this 'so called' community. Nearly all the gay people I know do not identify as LGBTQ+, in fact, they actively do not want to be associated with it for they think it is lunacy. Homosexuals have everything they have ever asked for, this fight is over, please go home if you are fighting for gay rights. The rest of the alphabet people need to work out what they want and let us know, for we do not care enough to try to work it out for ourselves. The British public is at 99% consensus that whatever consenting adults do in the privacy of their own home is none of it is our business – as long as it is legal. *Enjoy. Carry on. Fill your boots.* But stop forcing us to be part of it, accepting of it, and change our lives to accommodate it. Leave us alone and let us live our lives in peace.

Everything now comes under an umbrella term for all this nonsense, the word is *'woke.'* The first question I am asked when I use the word is what does it mean? The meaning has changed considerably since its first use in 1960s America.

My definition of 'woke': *political correctness on steroids with a little nastiness thrown in.*

Webster dictionary definition of 'woke': *to be aware of and actively attentive to important facts and issues, especially issues of racial and social justice.*

The biggest flaw of the *wokerati* is that they do not build or create anything, they only tear down and destroy. They are just new versions of bitter art critics and armchair football managers, they think they can do better without ever attempting to try. Creating the world we have today took thousands of years, it was not easy. Yet, any tattooed, blue-haired, 22-year-old Uni student with a dozen virginal piercings thinks she has the answer to poverty, unequal outcomes, and a fairer society. Really?

Stop looking for excuses, for they can always be found.

Stop accepting less than you know you are capable of.

Stop feeling sorry for yourself, it makes you weak.

Stop blaming others for the things that are in your hands.

Just stop pretending to be a victim.

Victim mentality produces beggars, victor mentality does not.

There comes a point where we need to stop just pulling people out of the river. We need to go upstream and find out why they're falling in.

- Archbishop Desmond Tutu

III. Final Words

Let us take a journey upstream and find out why people are falling in the river. This is a sensible action to discover the information we need if we are to solve the problem. What you discover may surprise you. Remember my chat with the homeless gents sitting on shopping baskets outside the supermarket?

No one really knows why humans do what they do.
- David K. Reynolds

Our strategy for the last half-century has been to throw a life ring into the water to save individuals from drowning. We do not drag them out of the river for this would mean we would get wet, muddy and dirty – we do not care that much. So we leave them bobbing up and down in the life ring in the shallow section of the river away from immediate danger and away from us. There is not much value in telling people struggling to swim that they should have made different choices in life and learnt how to doggy paddle. Pointing or wagging a finger at the feckless changes nothing. It may make you feel better for imparting your wisdom, but be careful, fingers can point in many directions.

Some businesses, charities and political careers have a vested interest in the status quo – follow the money, the power and the virtue signalling. Relative poverty is a growth industry for we are working hard for it to never stop, only grow. Where is the incentive for professionals to stop the perverse treatment of fellow citizens? They hide their inhumanity under a cloak of compassion, ribbons on their lapel and flags in their Twitter bio.

Can we all simply agree on what will stop people from falling into the river of despair and concentrate our efforts on a strategy that reduces the number of these accidents? Better education system. Hand-up welfare system. A criminal justice system that reduces crime. Employment that pays decent wages. A society that demands self-resilience. Citizens that accept personal responsibility.

We have allowed ourselves to decay and become weak. We have had it so good for so long that we are not able to accept reality and are afraid of our own shadows. We are not prepared to sacrifice any part of today for a better tomorrow. Our society is based around instant gratification, this type of behaviour used to be only found in children and the foolish.

Never forget that life is hard and unfair. We do not live in the world of our desire, but the world as it is – harsh and unforgiving. But as a species, we have come a long way from the days when we were at the mercy of the weather, disease and predators. We conquered and overcame. We were not beggars - we did not ask for something for nothing. We were fighters, explorers and inventors. We gave ourselves goals and we achieved them. We saw the tomorrow we wanted and went for it.

We spent thousands of years hunting the predators that were hunting us, this is why most dangerous animals keep away from us for they have learnt that we bring death and destruction. Eventually, we turned our attention to other humans as we competed for resources and power. The history of mankind is a history of atrocities. More recently, we have refocused our efforts back onto predators, but this time microorganisms that invade our bodies and kill us. *Smallpox. Tuberculous. Measles. HIV.* Look at our successful fight against the *Covid* pandemic – regardless of the mistakes incurred, what we put in place was miraculous. As a species, we have taken whatever the planet has thrown at us and been victorious for we are a formidable species.

As the British nation, we have also excelled. Our culture has seen us develop from a tiny insignificant island on the edge of nowhere to having the largest empire in the history of the world. So vast that '*the sun never set*' for we had sovereign territory in every corner of the globe. We ended the slave trade that had been seen as normal since the beginning of time. We gave the world democracy, a legal system, world trade and our greatest gift, the English language. We defeated fascism, communism and hopefully fundamental Islamism. We gave the world its favourite sports such as football, rugby, snooker, cricket, tennis and boxing. We invented the steam engine, the tin can, chocolate bars, the world wide web, public railway, vaccines and the mass production of stainless steel.

As a small nation, we have constantly punched above our weight and size. This is why it hurts me so much to see our once great nation on its knees with its hand out to the EU for a trade deal, to the USA for protection, to Russia and Saudi Arabia for energy, and to China for investment. Our leaders have relied on others to solve the problems we elected them to fix. It is plain to see that we are not producing the leaders we need, and it is entirely our own fault for we have the power of the ballot box.

In a democracy, people get the leaders they deserve.
- Joseph de Maistre

We have seen recently that our worldview is simply just a view. When the Russian tanks rolled across the Ukrainian border in 2022 we were shocked, for we thought we understood the world we live in, especially the European world. Military invasions, refugees, bombed-out cities, human carnage and mass panic were only visions from other continents, never from civilised Europe. We fail to remember the break up of Yugoslavia, the concentration camps, the atrocities and the war crime tribunals. Self-imposed amnesia seems to be the only way humans cope with the magnitude of possible threats we face on daily basis.

Russia has kindly reminded us that the world is not safe, not tolerant and not compassionate. This invasion is a wake-up call to us and the West in general. We cannot continue teaching our citizens that the world owes them a living, that they are somehow special, and their feelings matter. For none of this is true and is a pathetic stance to take. Remember the word '*fredsskadade*' from chapter 4? *Injured by peace.*

Our country will now be moving towards becoming energy self-sufficient so we do not have to rely on imported gas and oil from unfriendly, unstable or immoral nations. Our armed forces will be strengthened for we can all see a war coming, not with Russia for they are weak, but with the new global superpower: China. If war is avoided, it will be because the West collectively invested in its military and deterred the expansionist dreams of an authoritarian 'so called' communist regime. Taking national defence seriously today will deliver a safer tomorrow. Should you wait until you have been burgled before fitting a home alarm system or should you think ahead?

We need to deter our enemies. This is achieved by being formidable and not showing weakness. As well as being clear and concise so there is no confusion or room for misinterpretation. But most importantly, you need to understand that your most dangerous enemy is buried deep within you. Your only options are to conquer it or sign a peace treaty. You cannot live your life under constant attack suffering the sling and arrows of self-doubt, low self-esteem, and low self-worth. This leads to thoughts of giving up and this should never be an option for this is how beggars are made.

Everyone's goal should be self-sufficiency by gaining the skills needed in life. This includes earning your own money and owing allegiance to no one – except Queen and country.

For a better tomorrow, you must work hard today. You plant the seed of a tree as a child, so you have shade to rest under when old. It is never too late to start planning for tomorrow, most of us will live well into our 90s. Small changes today add up over time.

> *The fact that you woke up this morning is proof that this day has already been predetermined in your favour.* - **Russ Kyle**